THE
SPACE
RACE

Contents

Foreword

Being in space is awesome. It is the most amazing human experience. You can look out the window to see Earth, stretch out your arms and feel like you are flying over the planet. You can see fires burning, the wake of ships, and the different colours of the oceans. Sometimes you'll see snow, or the forest and jungles. Earth is so beautiful. But the most amazing thing is that you are floating!

I started getting interested in space when I was nine years old, reading about the Gemini astronauts during the space race. I wanted to be one of them. They were all men, but I never thought that I couldn't do it because I was a girl. I said to myself that's what I'm going to do – I'm going to be an astronaut. It was the ultimate flying job and I have always wanted to go farther and faster and higher. When Apollo astronauts walked on the Moon, I was reading books about flying.

My family had no money but I got a job at 16 and saved up to pay for flying lessons. Later, I became one of the first women to go through pilot training with the Air Force. In those days, women weren't allowed to fly in combat, but I was asked to stay as an instructor, so I got to fly fast jets – this gave me the experience needed to go to test pilot school and apply to be an astronaut.

When I was selected as the first woman to pilot the Space Shuttle, this also meant that I would have the opportunity to be a Commander one day. I knew that commanding a space mission would be the most important job I would ever do. At NASA, I decided to work as hard as I could to be the best that I could be. It was important to me to get along with people, be a good communicator, and to help people work together to achieve the goal of the mission.

I twice flew to space as a pilot and then, in 1999, I flew my first mission as a commander. I was the first woman to ever command a Space Shuttle mission. It was a huge honour and a huge responsibility.

My advice to you is to learn about the world. To explore. That is where you will discover what you want to do with your life. Listen to your teachers, and study maths, science, and engineering – these subjects are important for our future. Learning other languages is also important, because space exploration involves lots of countries.

I hope in the future we will see people on the surface of Mars. To get there, we will need to go back to the Moon, to test equipment. At the moment, 12 men have walked on the Moon. They did so between 1969 and 1972, but no woman has walked on the Moon. Women were certainly capable, but the culture at the time didn't allow women to do that. But we will definitely see the first woman walk on the Moon and we will see people walk on Mars.

My other hope is that we discover a way to travel faster in space, so we can go to the other planets in our Solar System and then eventually outside of our Solar System. A future discovery is awaiting us so that we will have the ability to do that. Maybe you will be part of inventing or discovering something like this in your lifetime.

Eileen M. Collins

Astronaut Eileen Collins
First female Space Shuttle Commander

It took one photo to change the way we viewed the world forever. This is our home, planet Earth, as seen from the Moon. Everything we have ever known has existed on this blue marble in the darkness of space. Every animal, plant, and person – everything.

For thousands of years, people looked out to space and developed tools, such as telescopes, to learn more about what was out there. They would dream about space travel, of one day reaching the stars, but it was only in the last century that those dreams started to become a reality.

Today we live in what is known as a space age. Some humans live and work in space and we are constantly making new discoveries. Space is exciting because we still don't know about everything that's out there. However, we do know that space contains many other planets. There are likely to be millions and millions of them. They are too far away for you to see with the naked eye, and we don't know if life exists on any of them.

We went to space because we were curious. We continue to go to space because we still have many unanswered questions about our Universe.

Earthrise
This photograph was taken by the crew of Apollo 8 on 24 December 1968. It is the first photo that a human took of the Earth from the Moon.

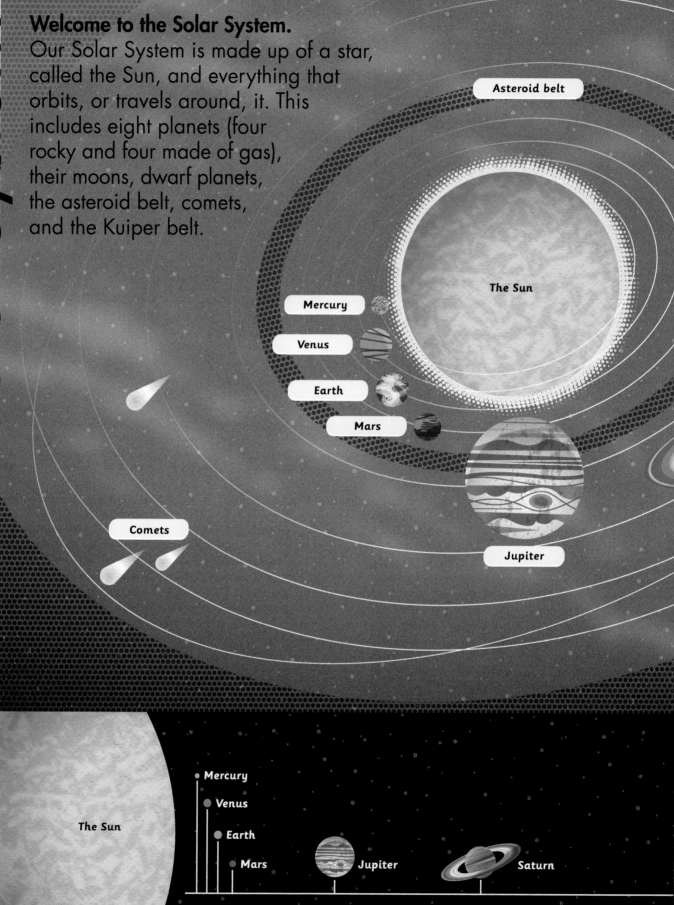

Our Solar System

Welcome to the Solar System.
Our Solar System is made up of a star, called the Sun, and everything that orbits, or travels around, it. This includes eight planets (four rocky and four made of gas), their moons, dwarf planets, the asteroid belt, comets, and the Kuiper belt.

Asteroid belt

The Sun

Mercury

Venus

Earth

Mars

Comets

Jupiter

The Sun

Mercury

Venus

Earth

Mars

Jupiter

Saturn

Pluto
The dwarf planet Pluto takes 248 Earth years to travel around the Sun!

Neptune

Uranus

Saturn

Kuiper belt
Millions of icy and rocky objects, including comets and dwarf planets, make up this region at the edge of the Solar System.

Distances
The distances between objects in space is huge. Earth is about 150 million km (93 million miles) from the Sun. Scientists call this distance one astronomical unit (AU).

Uranus

Neptune

Rocky planets
The four inner planets of our Solar System are known as rocky planets because they are mostly made of rock.

Mercury
The closest planet to the Sun, Mercury is a scorching-hot, rocky world with no air to breathe.

Venus
The second planet from the Sun has a choking-thick atmosphere that can crush spacecraft landing there.

Earth
Our home, Earth, is the third planet from the Sun and the fifth largest in the Solar System.

Mars
This planet is also known as the Red Planet due to the reddish rust (iron oxide) in its rocks.

Gas giants
The four outer planets are the largest in our Solar System. They are mostly made of gas, so spacecraft cannot land on them.

Jupiter
The biggest planet in our Solar System is so massive you could fit more than 1,300 Earths inside it!

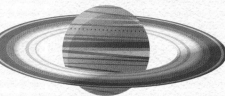

Saturn
This large planet is famous for its beautiful rings, which are made of rocks and ice.

Uranus
The oddball of the Solar System, Uranus orbits the Sun tilted on its side.

Neptune
The furthest planet from the Sun, Neptune is also the windiest place in our Solar System.

Our star, the Sun, is one of hundreds of billions of stars in a galaxy called the Milky Way. This galaxy is just one of many billions of galaxies in the Universe. There are so many stars and galaxies that no one would ever be able to count them all.

Solar System

Earth is part of the Solar System. It orbits, or moves around, the Sun, which is one of many stars in the Milky Way that has planets orbiting around it.

Earth

Our planet has all the ingredients needed for life to flourish. It is the perfect distance from the Sun to be just the right temperature and to have liquid water. At the moment, it is the only place we know for sure that has life on it.

Milky Way

Located in the Milky Way's outer spiral arm, our Solar System travels around its centre — known as the galactic centre. One orbit takes about 230 million years.

Universe of galaxies

This photograph was taken by the Hubble Space Telescope. Every shape you can see is a galaxy. These are just some of the many billions of galaxies in the Universe.

Stone Age
This cave painting was found in the Lascaux caves in southwestern France. It is more than 15,000 years old and was created during the Stone Age. It shows a cluster of six stars, known as the Pleiades, above the bull's shoulder.

Ancient Greece
The Greeks used to call planets "wanderering stars", as they looked like stars that moved across the sky. Ancient Greek astronomers were among the first people to study our Solar System.

Dreaming of space

On a clear night, you have probably looked at the night sky and wondered what was out there. Humans have always been fascinated by space.

Cave paintings, thousands of years old, provide the first records of people looking at the stars. Later, astronomers began studying space and creating maps of the night sky. During the Age of Exploration (1450–1750 CE), the oceans became the great frontier as we began to explore Earth, and sailors would use the Moon and the stars to navigate the seas.

As technology developed at the start of the 20th century, so did our dreams about space. Science-fiction writers imagined trips to the Moon and voyages to faraway worlds. However, the reality of going to space was still beyond our reach.

Star navigation
Sailors measured the positions of stars in the night sky to help them navigate. These star patterns helped sailors to work out which way was north, east, south, and west.

Ancient China
China has a long history of astronomy – the Chinese thought that the movement of stars in the sky showed the actions of their emperors. This Chinese star chart is the earliest known map of the night sky, and dates back to around 700 CE.

Science fiction
First published in 1898, *The War of the Worlds* by H.G. Wells captured the public's imagination with its tales of aliens and space travel.

Early dreams of space flight
In 1902, the French film *Le Voyage dans la Lune* (*A Trip to the Moon*) was released. It told the story of a group of astronomers who were blasted from a cannon on Earth all the way to the Moon.

Montgolfier balloons
The Montgolfier brothers invented the hot-air balloon in southern France. This creation signalled the start of air travel.

Up, up, and away!

Wright Flyer
The world's first successful aeroplane, the Wright Flyer, was made of wood with a fabric covering.

Before we could go to space, we had to conquer the skies. Some of the earliest attempts to fly, such as wearing wings to try to copy birds, had not ended very well.

The first breakthrough came in 1783, when a sheep, a duck, and a cockerel became the first passengers on a hot-air balloon flight. However, it wasn't until 17 December 1903 that two American brothers, Wilbur and Orville Wright, made the seemingly impossible possible. The brothers designed and flew the world's first successful aeroplane, the Wright Flyer. The first flight lasted just 12 seconds, but it inspired more people to try to fly aeroplanes.

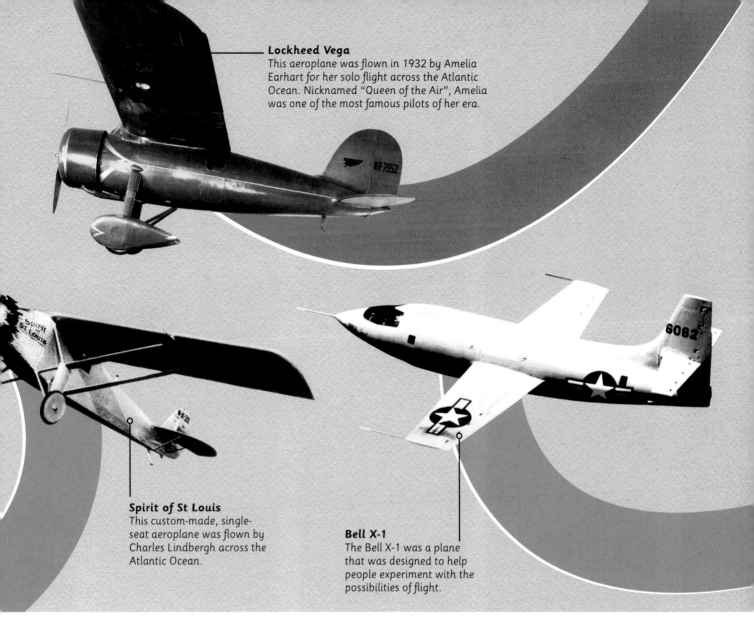

Lockheed Vega
This aeroplane was flown in 1932 by Amelia Earhart for her solo flight across the Atlantic Ocean. Nicknamed "Queen of the Air", Amelia was one of the most famous pilots of her era.

Spirit of St Louis
This custom-made, single-seat aeroplane was flown by Charles Lindbergh across the Atlantic Ocean.

Bell X-1
The Bell X-1 was a plane that was designed to help people experiment with the possibilities of flight.

A new era in exploration had begun. In 1927, Charles Lindbergh became the first person to fly from New York to Paris by aeroplane. Then in 1932, Amelia Earhart became the first woman to fly across the Atlantic Ocean alone.

During World War II, aircraft became larger and more powerful, as countries including the UK, USA, Germany, and Japan created new types of bomber, fighter, and transport plane. These developments led to the Bell X-1, which Chuck Yeager flew in 1947. The Bell X-1 was more like a space rocket than a plane, and it flew faster than the speed of sound! This rocket plane proved that space flight was almost a reality.

To travel to space, you need a powerful rocket. While rockets are modern inventions, the ideas behind them are thousands of years old.

One of the first people to think about rockets was the ancient Greek scientist and philosopher Archytas. He created a steam-powered wooden pigeon in around 400 BCE, which flew along a wire for 200 m (650 ft). The first real rockets came from China, where gunpowder was invented.

Archytas and his flying pigeon
Powered by steam, Archytas's flying pigeon was made from wood.

Rocket power

The Chinese put gunpowder in tubes, which then fired arrows when lit. These were used in battles in around 1200 CE.

However, it was not until the start of the 20th century that scientists began to think about rockets flying to space. During World War II, engineers in Nazi Germany, led by rocket scientist Wernher von Braun, developed the V-2 rocket. This was a long-range missile that was so powerful it could travel to the edge of space.

Chinese fire arrows
These worked using gunpowder, which, when lit, pushed gas, fire, and smoke out of one end to move the arrow forwards.

Konstantin Tsiolkovsky
In 1903, the maths equations needed for rocket travel were developed by the Soviet engineer Konstantin Tsiolkovsky.

How rockets work

The basic principles behind rockets are fairly simple. Burning rocket fuel releases gases that push the rocket skywards. To work, the rocket has a hole in the base for the gas to escape from, and a smooth, shaped top so that it can easily glide through the air and not be slowed down.

Reaction
The rocket reacts to the power of the gas being pushed out of the back by moving upwards.

Action
Pushing the gas out of the bottom of the engine makes the rocket move forwards.

Robert Goddard
In the late 1920s, American engineer Robert Goddard launched the world's first liquid-fuelled rocket. He laid the foundations for modern rocketry, and proved that rockets would be able to work in space.

Robert Esnault-Pelterie
In the 1930s, French engineer Robert Esnault-Pelterie experimented with different types of rocket. In one experiment he lost some of his fingers in an explosion!

Hermann Oberth
The German physicist and engineer Hermann Oberth (centre) was inspired by science fiction. His work showed how rockets could escape the Earth's gravity.

V-2 rocket
First flown in 1942, the German V-2 rocket was used as a weapon in World War II. It also showed that it was possible to use a rocket to get to space.

Von Braun

During World War II, the United States and the Soviet Union fought together on the same side. However, after the war ended in 1945, a new conflict between the two nations arose – the Cold War. This was unlike anything the world had seen before. It was a clash of two hugely powerful countries.

The United States and the Soviet Union didn't ever actually fight during the Cold War. Instead, both nations wanted to increase their influence around the world and show that their way of life was the best. Going to space was one way to do this, and they needed the best rocket engineers to help achieve their goals: Wernher von Braun and Sergei Korolev.

Both countries started perfecting their spacecraft technology. After World War II, some of the engineers

Wernher von Braun 1912–1977

From a young age, German-born Wernher von Braun was interested in space travel. He was inspired by the rocket pioneer Hermann Oberth. Von Braun became a famous figure in the United States for his work at NASA.

VS
Korolev

who built the German V-2 rocket travelled east to the Soviet Union. Many others, including von Braun, the German inventor of the V-2 rocket, went to the United States. After relocating, von Braun and his team began to develop rockets for the US Army. They later moved to the newly formed National Aeronautics and Space Administration (NASA).

Meanwhile, in the Soviet Union, the efforts to get to space were led by Korolev. A rocket engineer and designer, Korolev started the Soviet space programme, leading the designs of its spacecraft. In the summer of 1955, the United States announced its plans to send a satellite into space. A few days later, the Soviet Union said it would do the same. The space race had begun.

Sergei Korolev 1907–1966

Born in present-day Ukraine, Sergei Korolev had originally trained as an aircraft designer. He was the mastermind behind the Soviet Union's rockets. At the time, his name was kept secret from the rest of the world.

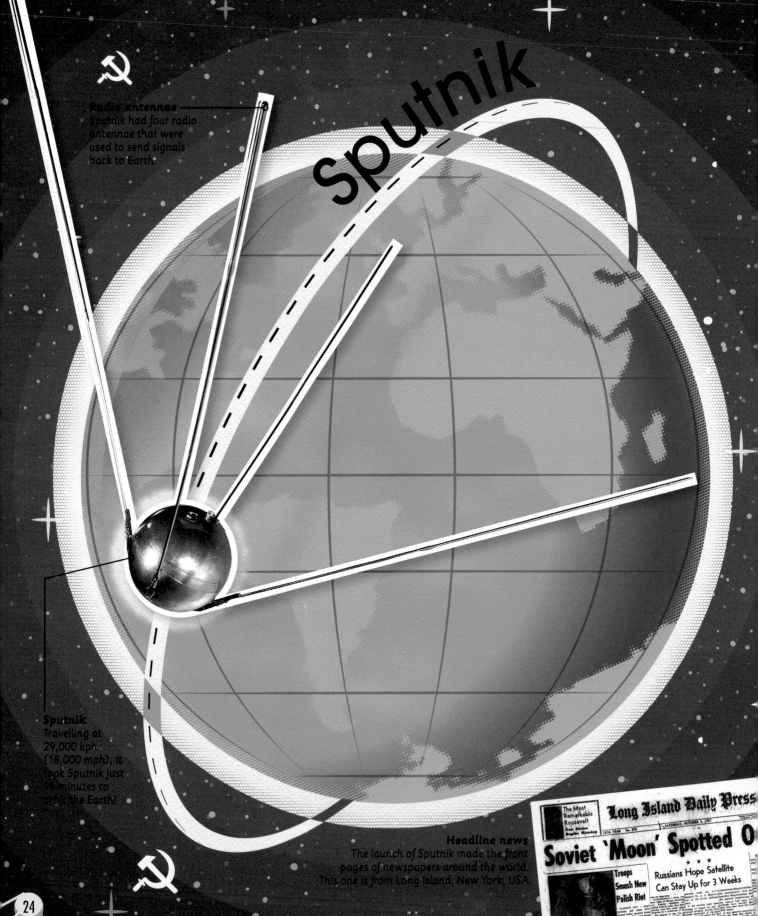

Sputnik

Radio antennae
Sputnik had four radio antennae that were used to send signals back to Earth.

Sputnik
Travelling at 29,000 kph (18,000 mph), it took Sputnik just 96 minutes to orbit the Earth!

Headline news
The launch of Sputnik made the front pages of newspapers around the world. This one is from Long Island, New York, USA.

Long Island Daily Press

Soviet 'Moon' Spotted O

Troops Smash New Polish Riot

Russians Hope Satellite Can Stay Up for 3 Weeks

The Most Remarkable Roosevelt

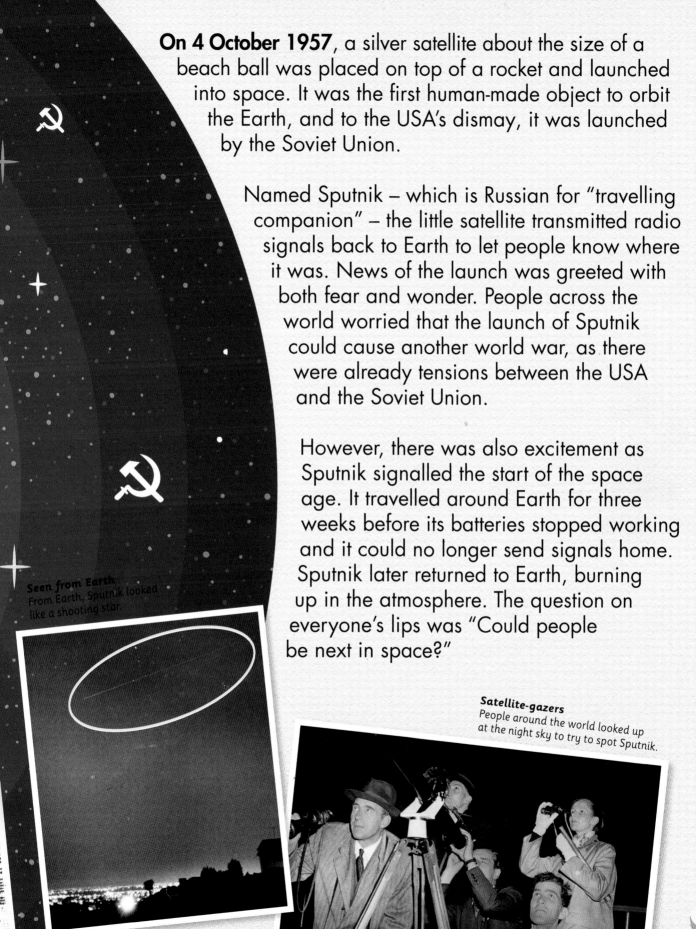

On 4 October 1957, a silver satellite about the size of a beach ball was placed on top of a rocket and launched into space. It was the first human-made object to orbit the Earth, and to the USA's dismay, it was launched by the Soviet Union.

Named Sputnik – which is Russian for "travelling companion" – the little satellite transmitted radio signals back to Earth to let people know where it was. News of the launch was greeted with both fear and wonder. People across the world worried that the launch of Sputnik could cause another world war, as there were already tensions between the USA and the Soviet Union.

However, there was also excitement as Sputnik signalled the start of the space age. It travelled around Earth for three weeks before its batteries stopped working and it could no longer send signals home. Sputnik later returned to Earth, burning up in the atmosphere. The question on everyone's lips was "Could people be next in space?"

Seen from Earth
From Earth, Sputnik looked like a shooting star.

Satellite-gazers
People around the world looked up at the night sky to try to spot Sputnik.

25

Laika's mission

Laika's journey around Earth in the Sputnik 2 capsule led to more successful flights for dogs, and eventually humans. Unfortunately, Laika's mission ended in space as she died while in orbit.

Animals in space

Animals paved the way for humans to go to space. Scientists did not know if a person could survive a trip to space, and if they could, what would happen to the human body.

They decided to send animals to space first, to test the impact that space travel would have on a living being. This testing began shortly after World War II, and in 1947 the Americans used a German V-2 rocket to send fruit flies to space. During the late 1940s and early 1950s, different types of small creatures, such as mice, were launched to high altitudes. One of the most famous animal explorers was a stray dog from the Soviet Union called Laika. On 3 November 1957, she became the first animal to orbit the Earth.

Chimps were also sent to space, including one called Ham. He was trained to pull a series of levers in the correct order in exchange for a reward of banana pellets. NASA wanted to see whether it was possible for Ham to complete tasks when he was weightless in the microgravity of space. In total, Ham's space mission lasted 16 minutes.

Ham's mission

Ham was just three years old when he was launched into space in January 1961. The mission earned him the nickname "Astrochimp". After returning from space, Ham retired to the National Zoo in Washington, D.C., USA.

Introducing...
The Mercury 7

Meet Alan, Gus, Gordon, Wally, Deke, John, and Scott. In 1959, they became some of the most famous people in the world – America's first astronauts, nicknamed the Mercury 7.

The Mercury 7 had been selected from a group of more than 100 elite military test pilots. They were skilled at flying different types of aircraft and could think fast in dangerous situations. This group of seven had shown that they had what it took to go to space. They had to pass lots of tests, which were designed to reproduce what scientists thought might happen to a person who travelled to space. Also, they had to be a maximum of 1.8 m (5 ft 11 in) tall because they had to fit inside a tiny spacecraft.

Their mission was Project Mercury, the NASA programme to put an astronaut in space ahead of the Soviet Union. The programme was named after the Roman god Mercury, who was known for being fast. They were the best of the best, and they were now American heroes.

Alan Shepard

Wally Schirra

Gus Grissom

Gordon Cooper

Deke Slayton

John Glenn

Scott Carpenter

Yuri Gagarin

The first person to travel to space, Yuri Gagarin, is seen here holding a dove, which is a symbol of peace. On the right is a photograph of his launch into space aboard his Vostok 1 spacecraft.

The first humans in space

On 12 April 1961, there was a breakthrough in the space race. For the first time in the history of humanity, a person left Earth and travelled to space. That person was cosmonaut Yuri Gagarin, a 27-year-old fighter pilot from the Soviet Union.

That morning, Yuri had put on his spacesuit before riding a bus to the launch pad in a place called Baikonur, Kazakhstan. He then climbed inside a tiny spacecraft on top of a rocket. The clock began to count down, and just before the launch Yuri yelled "Let's go!" Minutes later he was in space. Among those watching was rocket inventor Sergei Korolev, who was so nervous he couldn't sleep the night before.

Yuri flew around the Earth at a speed of 8 kilometres per second (5 miles per second) and travelled more than 320 km (200 miles) above the Earth, which was higher than any human had ever been before. He was the first person to see Earth from space and the first person to experience being weightless – although there was not enough room to float around in his tiny spacecraft.

Launch traditions

On the day of his launch, Yuri did a wee on the back tyres of the bus that was taking him to the launch pad! It has become a tradition for cosmonauts travelling to space from Baikonur to do the same.

One hour and 48 minutes later, and having completed one orbit of our planet, Yuri returned safely to Earth. In the Soviet Union, he was welcomed back as a hero, while the United States was in shock – they had been beaten once again.

The Americans

On 5 May 1961, Alan Shepard became the first American, and second person, to travel to space, only a few weeks after Yuri. However, his spaceflight lasted just 15 minutes. It took until February 1962 for an American – John Glenn – to orbit the Earth.

The race for the Moon

"We **choose** to go to the Moon! We choose to go to the Moon in **this decade** and do the other things, not because they are easy, but because they are hard."
– John F. Kennedy

On 25 May 1961, US President John F. Kennedy presented a new idea to his government. He wanted to send a human to the Moon and return them safely to Earth before the end of the decade. Up to this point, the United States had only sent an astronaut into space for 15 minutes, so landing on the Moon seemed almost impossible.

In September of the same year, President Kennedy gave an iconic speech to 40,000 people in Houston, Texas. He stated his goal to achieve a human Moon landing before the Soviet Union. At this time, space travel was very new and mysterious. The Americans knew that the Soviet Union was leading the space race by sending the first person to space – Yuri Gagarin – and so something extraordinary had to be done to get ahead.

President Kennedy came up with the idea of going to the Moon because it was something that the Soviet Union could not do with their existing rockets. The United States had advanced spacecraft technology, and NASA confirmed that President Kennedy's goal was achievable.

Leading rocket designer Wernher von Braun now had the chance to make his dream of sending humans further into space a reality. Along with a huge team at NASA, and other engineers across the country, von Braun took on the difficult task of designing the rocket that would take the first humans to the Moon.

The Moon's orbit

The Moon takes just over 27 days to orbit the Earth. It travels around the Earth in an elliptical, or oval, shape. On average, the Moon is about 384,400 km (238,855 miles) away from the Earth.

The perigee is when the Moon is at its closest point to the Earth.

Earth

Moon

The apogee is when the Moon is at its furthest point from the Earth.

Valentina Tereshkova

While the United States set its sights on reaching the Moon, the Soviet Union continued to set new records in spaceflight. On 16 June 1963, cosmonaut Valentina Tereshkova became the first woman to travel to space.

Valentina spent three days orbiting the Earth alone in her Vostok capsule. Her call sign, which she used to identify herself on radio transmissions, was *Chayka*, meaning "Seagull". Back home, people watched video footage of her smiling with her log book floating in front of her.

Her spaceflight was part of a duel mission. Another cosmonaut, Valery Bykovsky, had travelled in a separate capsule that launched two days earlier.

The mission was a dream come true for Valentina, who was already a skilled parachute jumper. She returned to Earth a global icon, and later gained a doctorate in engineering.

Training for space

It took 18 months for Valentina to be ready for her spaceflight. She had to undergo lots of training, including tests to see how well she would cope with being on her own in space.

Valentina was wired up to machines for health checks.

This spinning frame (gyroscope) produced a sensation similar to tumbling in space.

Valentina studied engineering to learn how space rockets worked.

First spaceships

The first spaceships were extremely tiny. They could only fit one person inside and there wasn't much room to move around. There was nowhere to sleep, nowhere to wash, and there were no toilets. Luckily, the first space missions didn't last very long.

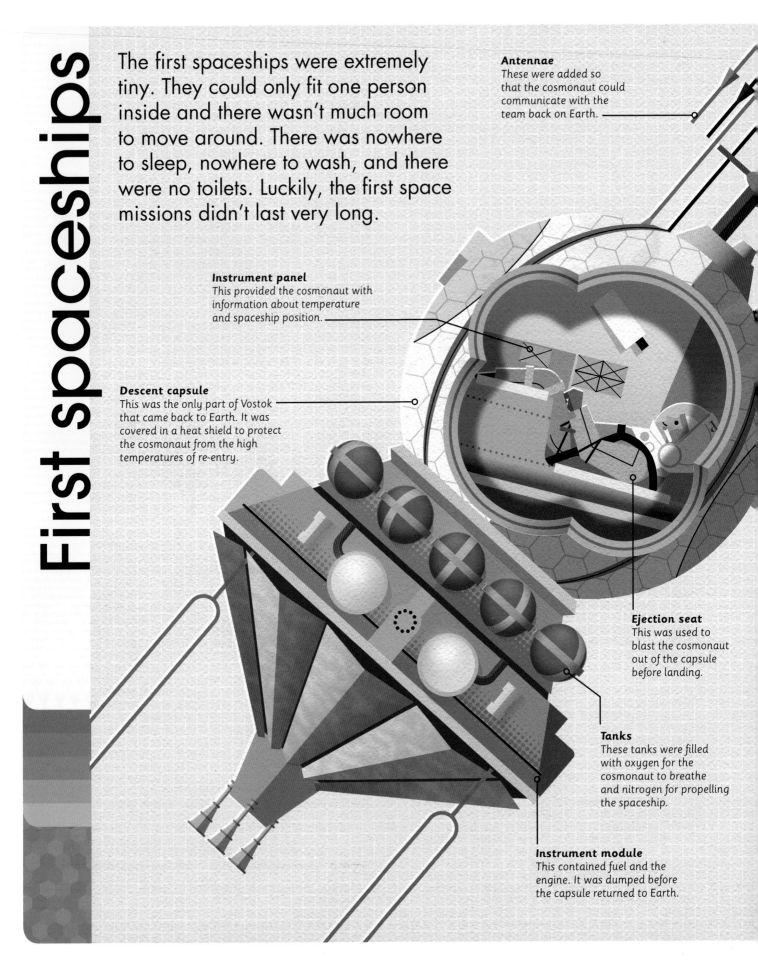

Antennae
These were added so that the cosmonaut could communicate with the team back on Earth.

Instrument panel
This provided the cosmonaut with information about temperature and spaceship position.

Descent capsule
This was the only part of Vostok that came back to Earth. It was covered in a heat shield to protect the cosmonaut from the high temperatures of re-entry.

Ejection seat
This was used to blast the cosmonaut out of the capsule before landing.

Tanks
These tanks were filled with oxygen for the cosmonaut to breathe and nitrogen for propelling the spaceship.

Instrument module
This contained fuel and the engine. It was dumped before the capsule returned to Earth.

Vostok

The Soviet Union used the Vostok spacecraft to send their first cosmonauts into space. It was first used in 1961 for Yuri Gagarin's mission.

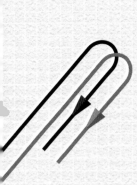

Vostok return mission

As if going to space was not daring enough, the first cosmonauts had to eject from their spacecraft as they returned to Earth and parachute down to the ground. This was because Vostok's landing was so violent, it could have injured the cosmonaut.

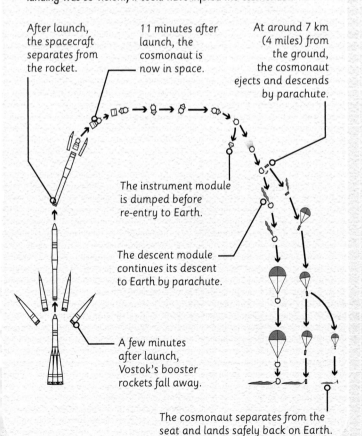

After launch, the spacecraft separates from the rocket.

11 minutes after launch, the cosmonaut is now in space.

At around 7 km (4 miles) from the ground, the cosmonaut ejects and descends by parachute.

The instrument module is dumped before re-entry to Earth.

The descent module continues its descent to Earth by parachute.

A few minutes after launch, Vostok's booster rockets fall away.

The cosmonaut separates from the seat and lands safely back on Earth.

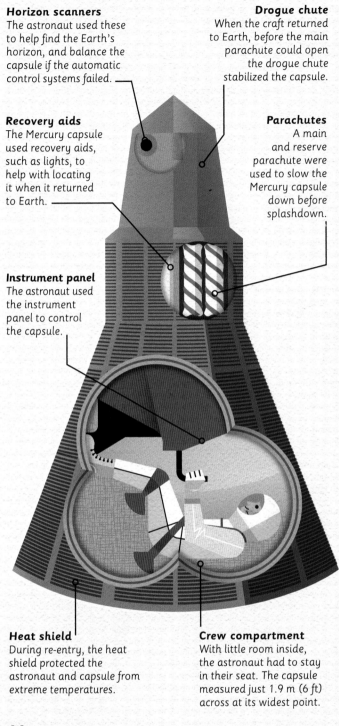

Horizon scanners
The astronaut used these to help find the Earth's horizon, and balance the capsule if the automatic control systems failed.

Recovery aids
The Mercury capsule used recovery aids, such as lights, to help with locating it when it returned to Earth.

Instrument panel
The astronaut used the instrument panel to control the capsule.

Drogue chute
When the craft returned to Earth, before the main parachute could open the drogue chute stabilized the capsule.

Parachutes
A main and reserve parachute were used to slow the Mercury capsule down before splashdown.

Heat shield
During re-entry, the heat shield protected the astronaut and capsule from extreme temperatures.

Crew compartment
With little room inside, the astronaut had to stay in their seat. The capsule measured just 1.9 m (6 ft) across at its widest point.

Mercury

NASA's Mercury space capsule was designed to splash down in the ocean after returning to Earth. The capsule was used for six crewed space missions, the first of which was in 1961. The longest mission was with Gordon Cooper, who spent more than 34 hours cramped inside and orbited the Earth 22 times!

Walking in space

Spacesuit problem

During Alexei Leonov's spacewalk, his spacesuit overinflated, making him too big to get back inside the airlock. In order to fit, Alexei decided to release some of the oxygen from inside the suit by opening a valve. His quick thinking prevented a disaster!

CCCP

This self-portrait shows Alexei in his spacesuit with the tether that was used to stop him floating away.

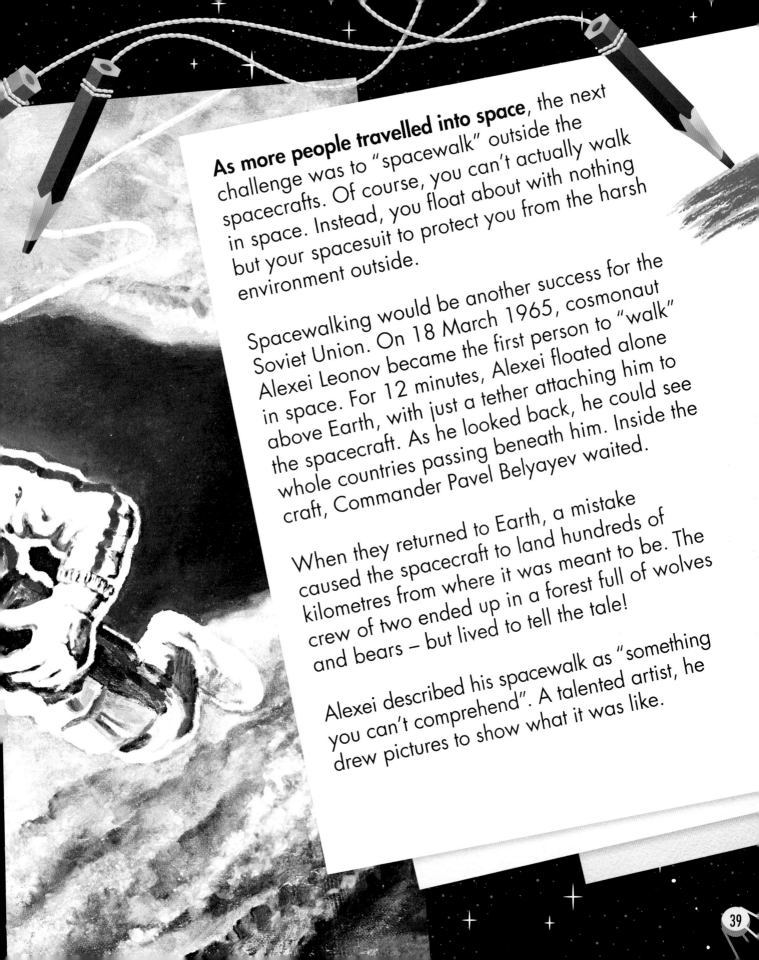

As more people travelled into space, the next challenge was to "spacewalk" outside the spacecrafts. Of course, you can't actually walk in space. Instead, you float about with nothing but your spacesuit to protect you from the harsh environment outside.

Spacewalking would be another success for the Soviet Union. On 18 March 1965, cosmonaut Alexei Leonov became the first person to "walk" in space. For 12 minutes, Alexei floated alone above Earth, with just a tether attaching him to the spacecraft. As he looked back, he could see whole countries passing beneath him. Inside the craft, Commander Pavel Belyayev waited.

When they returned to Earth, a mistake caused the spacecraft to land hundreds of kilometres from where it was meant to be. The crew of two ended up in a forest full of wolves and bears – but lived to tell the tale!

Alexei described his spacewalk as "something you can't comprehend". A talented artist, he drew pictures to show what it was like.

Project Gemini

To get to the Moon, NASA needed to learn lots of new skills, so it created Project Gemini. Gemini would send two astronauts into space at a time. There, they would learn to spacewalk, dock with other spacecraft, and spend longer in space than ever before.

In March 1966, Gemini 8, piloted by Neil Armstrong and Dave Scott, conducted the first ever docking of two spacecraft in orbit. However, after successfully docking with the uncrewed Agena Target Vehicle, their spacecraft began spinning wildly out of control.

The astronauts were in serious danger, but the quick thinking of Neil Armstrong saved the day. Despite spinning so fast his vision was going blurry, Neil managed to get the spacecraft back under control, aborted the mission, and returned them safely to Earth. Neil's amazing skills as a pilot would not go unnoticed.

Gemini 8 crew
First-time astronauts Dave Scott (left) and Neil Armstrong (right) pose with a model of the Gemini spacecraft.

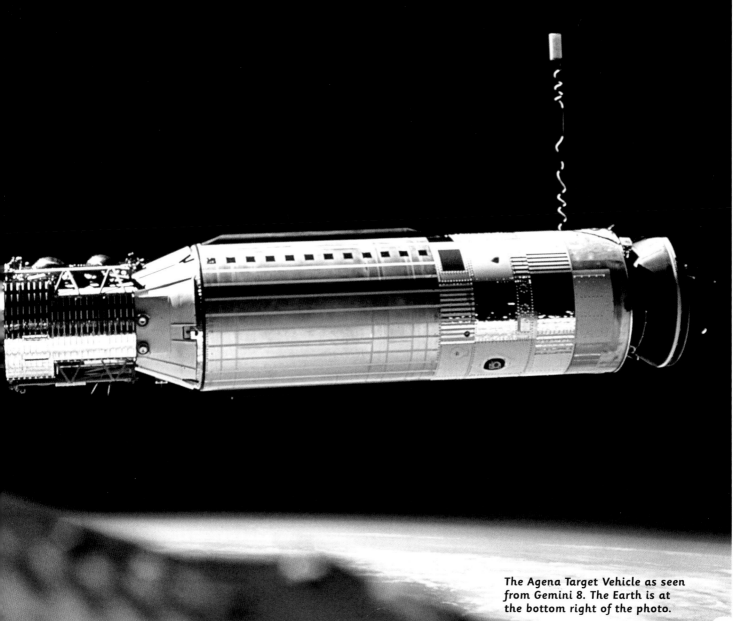

First American spacewalk

On 3 June 1965, Ed White became the first American to spacewalk. He spent 23 minutes floating in space tethered to his Gemini capsule. He was able to move around by using a hand-held oxygen jet gun.

The Agena Target Vehicle as seen from Gemini 8. The Earth is at the bottom right of the photo.

Rocket women

During the space race, all of the American astronauts were men, but women wanted to go to space too. A group of top female pilots undertook the same medical testing as the male NASA astronauts during a privately funded experiment. They had water injected in their ears and were locked in isolation tanks during gruelling mental and physical challenges.

Although 13 passed the tests, they couldn't continue with their dream of going to space because astronauts were required to fly jets, and at the time only men could do that. These pioneering women campaigned to let the testing continue, but with no luck. Among them was Irene Leverton, a well-known aviator of the time who had grown up wanting to fly fighter planes.

However, in 1995 astronaut Eileen Collins turned their dream into a reality when she became the first American woman to pilot a spacecraft. These 13 rocket women may not have been successful with their personal ambitions, but they paved the way for future female astronauts.

Jerrie Cobb
Jerrie poses next to the Mercury spaceship capsule. She was the first woman to complete the tests.

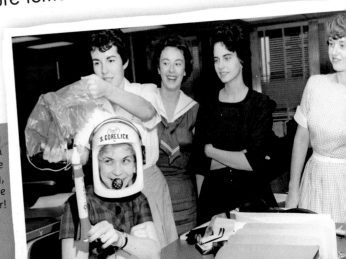

Testing
Some of the women during testing. On the left is Sarah Ratley, who could fly before she could drive a car!

Who were they?

Rhea Hurrle

Myrtle Cagle

Jerrie Cobb

Shuttle launch
Eileen Collins invited the women to watch her launch into space on 3 February 1995.

Janet Dietrich

Marion Dietrich

Wally Funk

Janey Hart

Jean Hixson

Sarah Gorelick

Irene Leverton

Jerri Sloan

Bernice Steadman

Gene Nora Stumbough

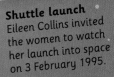

An interview with Sarah Ratley (née Gorelick)

Q. What was your background in flying?
A. I started flying while in high school and continued working in aviation after college, while being employed full-time in engineering.

Q. Why did you take part in the testing?
A. I was one of the very active women pilots at the time and my name was submitted to Dr Lovelace.

Q. How difficult was it?
A. The tests were a complete physical and mental examination, but I was determined to pass.

Q. What happened afterwards?
A. I continued to be active in aviation and hoped the programme would continue.

Q. What are your hopes for the future of the space programme?
A. The space programme has brought many new inventions and discoveries that help us in our daily lives. As we continue to explore, our quality of life will continue to improve.

Living in a space age

The start of the space race was a very exciting time on Earth. People were no longer just dreaming about space, they imagined a future in space. Space began to influence much of everyday life, from the clothes people wore to the food they ate and the toys children played with.

Toy rocket
Suddenly every child wanted a toy rocket like this one!

Technology
A futuristic makeover was given to technology around the home. For example, rectangular TVs began to be replaced with smooth, oval-shaped ones.

Tang
American astronauts drank Tang in space, as it was powdered and easy to make – you just add water! It became popular on Earth as people wanted to drink the same thing as astronauts.

Furniture
This chair was made by the Danish designer Verner Panton in 1965. It uses the smooth lines and colours found in furniture designed during the space age era.

TV shows
The Jetsons, a cartoon, showed life in a space age future, with flying cars, robot helpers, and camping trips to the Moon.

Ticket to space
People were so enthusiastic about space that the airline Pan Am began issuing tickets for trips to the Moon.

Know All Ye by These Presents that

has become a certified member of Pan Am's

"FIRST MOON FLIGHTS" CLUB

5893
Number

Vice President, Sales

FIRST SPACESHIP ON VENUS
TOTALVISION · TECHNICOLOR

THIS IS A FIRST! FANTASTIC! UNFORGETTABLE!

starring
YOKO TANI
OLDRICK LUKES
Directed by KURT MAETZIG
Written by JAMES FETHKE
A CENTRALA PRODUCTION

YOU ARE THERE...ON MAN'S MOST EXCITING, MOST INCREDIBLE JOURNEY!!

Sci-fi films
Movies were inspired by the space race, telling stories of people visiting other planets in the Solar System.

World's Fair
In 1964, the World's Fair in New York City, USA, showcased a future where space-age technology would improve life for everyone on Earth.

Toy robot
Children imagined a future where robots would help us explore space.

LOST IN SPACE ROBOT
OFFICIAL
BATTERY OPERATED

Fashion
Designers found inspiration in the space race. They created outfits that looked like they might be worn in space were people ever to move there.

Training for the Moon

Reduced gravity walking

On Earth, gravity keeps you on the ground, but there is far less gravity on the Moon. NASA helped astronauts to experience what less gravity would feel like by using a reduced gravity walking simulator.

Geology training

Moonwalkers needed to learn about geology. This would help them find the best samples of rocks and soil to bring back to Earth for scientists to study.

Overcoming tragedy

On 27 January 1967, disaster struck. A fire on the launch pad killed Gus Grissom, Edward White, and Roger Chaffee — the crew of Apollo 1. It took more than 18 months for NASA to successfully send people to space again. The lessons learned from Apollo 1 helped NASA to prevent any American astronauts dying in space during the Apollo missions.

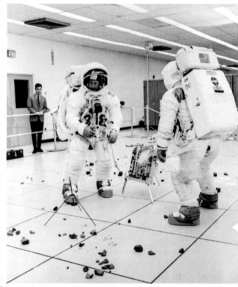

Training underwater

To be an astronaut you have to be able to swim. This is for when your spacecraft lands on water, and also because underwater training is a useful way for astronauts to practise what it would be like to perform a spacewalk. Here, astronaut Ken Mattingly is seen learning how to exit a spacecraft.

LLRV

The LLRV (Lunar Landing Research Vehicle) looked like a four-legged, flying bedframe. It was incredibly difficult to fly and was used to simulate descending to the surface of the Moon.

Tools

Working on the Moon, astronauts would need to use lots of different tools. Before going to space, they learned how to use drills, hammers, and scoops while inside their bulky suits.

EVA training

Lunar EVA (Extra Vehicular Activity) training helped to simulate what it would be like to work on the Moon. Astronauts in full kit rehearsed collecting samples and learned how to set up experiments.

Project LOLA

Project LOLA (Lunar Orbit and Landing Approach) was designed to show what it would be like to approach the Moon from space. During training, astronauts would move along a track going past a giant, hand-painted model of the surface of the Moon.

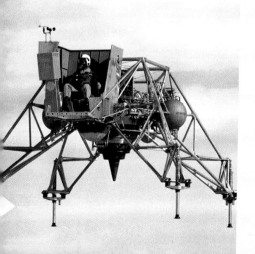

Water landing

The Apollo Command Module was designed to land on water once it came back from the Moon. Astronauts had to learn how to safely climb out of the spacecraft. In this photograph, they are seen practising in a swimming pool.

To get to the Moon, you need a gigantic rocket. The Americans built the Saturn V – a type of rocket known as a heavy lift launch vehicle. It was the most powerful rocket that had ever flown, capable of taking astronauts not only into Earth orbit but also to the Moon.

Super size

The huge Saturn V rocket was 111 m (363 ft) tall. That's more than the height of the Statue of Liberty and the base it stands on.

Saturn V

Statue of Liberty

Saturn V

The rocket was made up of three parts, or stages. The stages all contained fuel and burned in order. As each stage used up its fuel, it separated from the rest of the rocket. The first stage lifted the fully fuelled rocket off the ground. The second carried it until it was almost in Earth orbit. The third stage took it into Earth orbit and onwards to the Moon.

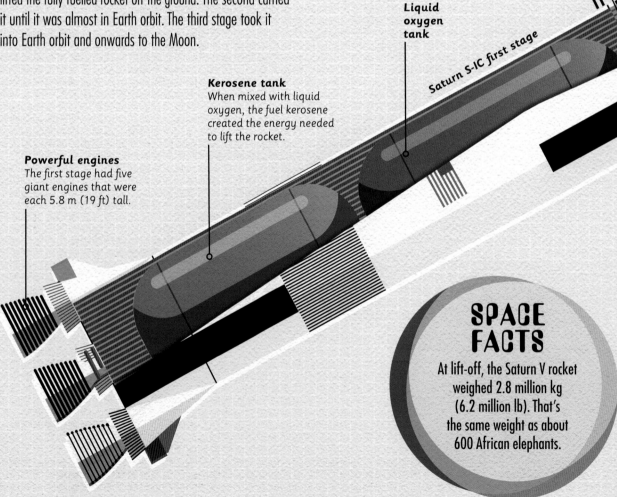

Five engines

Liquid oxygen tank

Saturn S-IC first stage

Kerosene tank
When mixed with liquid oxygen, the fuel kerosene created the energy needed to lift the rocket.

Powerful engines
The first stage had five giant engines that were each 5.8 m (19 ft) tall.

SPACE FACTS

At lift-off, the Saturn V rocket weighed 2.8 million kg (6.2 million lb). That's the same weight as about 600 African elephants.

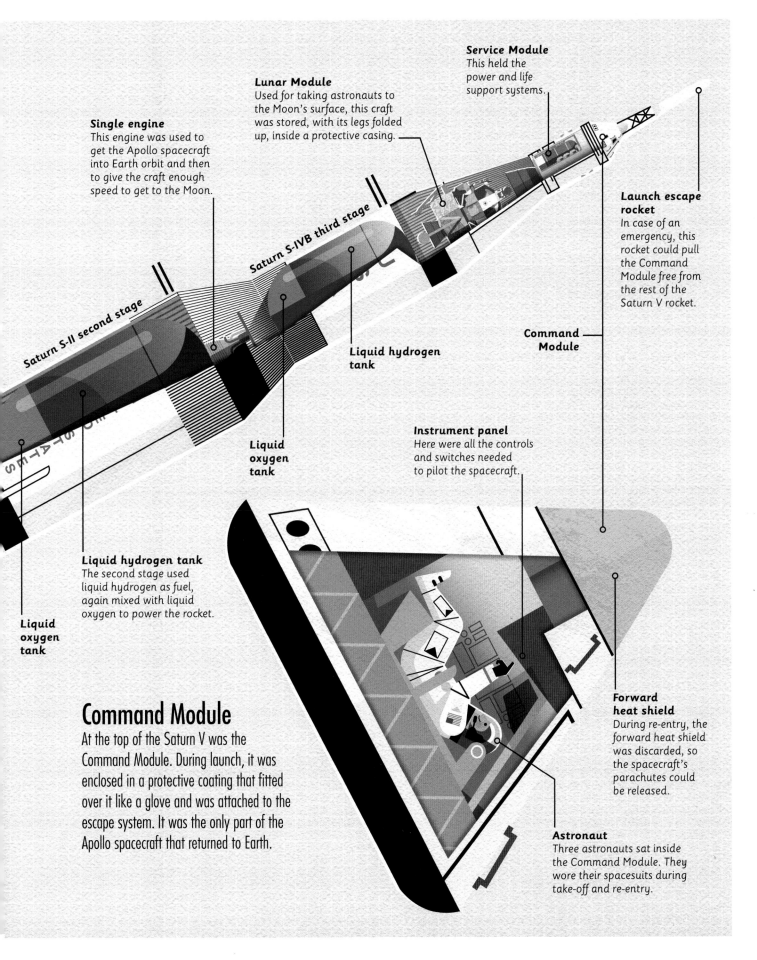

Single engine
This engine was used to get the Apollo spacecraft into Earth orbit and then to give the craft enough speed to get to the Moon.

Lunar Module
Used for taking astronauts to the Moon's surface, this craft was stored, with its legs folded up, inside a protective casing.

Service Module
This held the power and life support systems.

Saturn S-IVB third stage

Saturn S-II second stage

Liquid hydrogen tank

Launch escape rocket
In case of an emergency, this rocket could pull the Command Module free from the rest of the Saturn V rocket.

Command Module

Liquid oxygen tank

Instrument panel
Here were all the controls and switches needed to pilot the spacecraft.

Liquid hydrogen tank
The second stage used liquid hydrogen as fuel, again mixed with liquid oxygen to power the rocket.

Liquid oxygen tank

Command Module

At the top of the Saturn V was the Command Module. During launch, it was enclosed in a protective coating that fitted over it like a glove and was attached to the escape system. It was the only part of the Apollo spacecraft that returned to Earth.

Forward heat shield
During re-entry, the forward heat shield was discarded, so the spacecraft's parachutes could be released.

Astronaut
Three astronauts sat inside the Command Module. They wore their spacesuits during take-off and re-entry.

Slow-mo giants

The Crawler is a vehicle
with an important job at
NASA. It safely transports space
rockets from the Vehicle Assembly
Building (VAB) to the launch pad, and it
has a top speed of just 1.5 kph (1 mph) when
loaded. This journey is the last time that a rocket
is moved before it blasts into space.

NASA has two Crawlers, which were both built to transport
the Saturn V mega-rocket. However, they have been used for
lots of space missions since Apollo. The name "Crawler" comes
from the fact that it crawls very slowly along the road.

As well as being really slow, the crawlers are also huge. Each crawler is
34 m (113 ft) wide, and even without a space rocket onboard they weigh
nearly 2,700 tonnes (3,000 tons). They are truly slow-mo giants.

The Crawler

The Crawler is operated by a team of nearly 30 drivers, engineers, and technicians who drive it at really slow speeds. The cabin at the front is where the driver sits. In this photograph you can see people standing on the Crawler, which shows you just how big it is. Its size is very important as it needs to be big enough and strong enough to carry a space rocket!

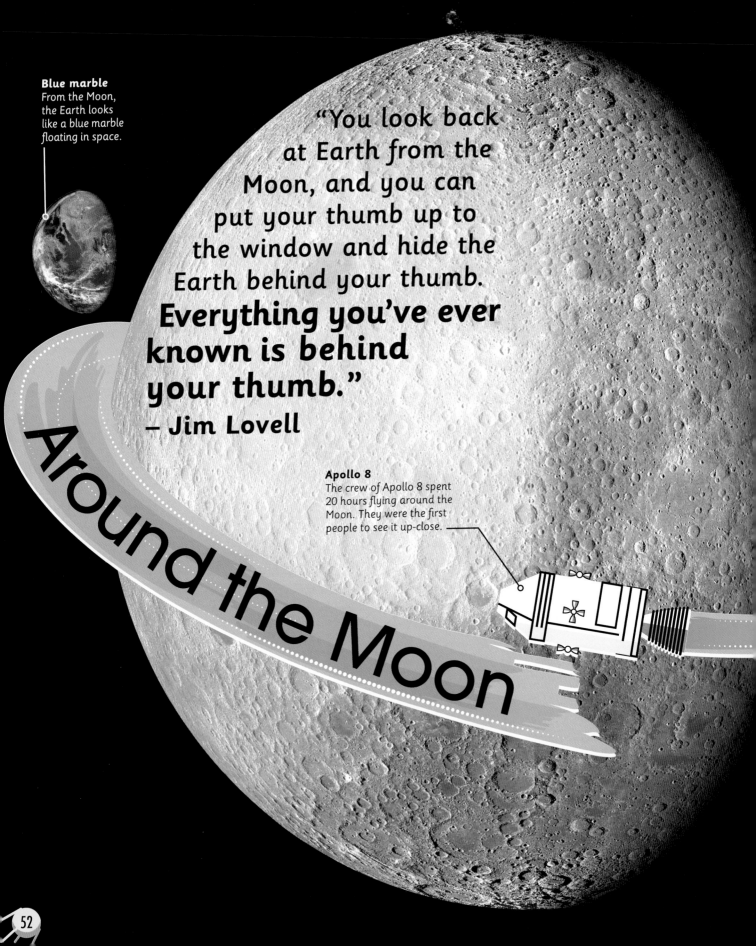

Blue marble
From the Moon, the Earth looks like a blue marble floating in space.

"You look back at Earth from the Moon, and you can put your thumb up to the window and hide the Earth behind your thumb. **Everything you've ever known is behind your thumb.**"
– Jim Lovell

Apollo 8
The crew of Apollo 8 spent 20 hours flying around the Moon. They were the first people to see it up-close.

Around the Moon

In 1968, fearing the Soviet Union would get there first, NASA decided to send three astronauts around the Moon and then return them to Earth. The mission was called Apollo 8. Commander Frank Borman, Bill Anders, and Jim Lovell would travel further into space than ever before, seeing the Moon from a height of just 111 km (69 miles).

The mission was extremely risky and in order to succeed everything had to work perfectly. On Christmas Eve 1968, the three astronauts arrived at the Moon. As they orbited around it they became the first people to see the far side of the Moon. Then, as they edged towards the near side, they saw the most awe-inspiring sight in human history – the Earth "rising" over the Moon's horizon.

Three days later the crew successfully returned to Earth. Their mission sent shockwaves across the Soviet Union. Up until then, they had been first to do everything in space, but now the Americans were ahead.

The crew of Apollo 8. From left to right: Jim Lovell, Bill Anders, and Frank Borman.

This photograph shows Earth rising above the Moon. Taken on 24 December 1968, it's called "Earthrise".

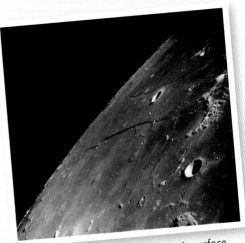

This is a photograph of the Moon's surface, taken by the crew of Apollo 8.

Mission control

Behind every space mission is the team working at mission control.

At NASA, once a rocket has blasted off, responsibility for the mission is given to the Mission Control Center in Houston, Texas, USA. Mission control is home to a team of experts who are involved with every part of a space mission – from planning and directing launches to guiding astronauts on spacewalks and helping with experiments in space. The people in mission control are supported by another team called the backroom staff, who help them make decisions in the event of a problem.

During the space race, the Soviet Union had their own version of mission control, though details of it were kept secret.

Chris Kraft
A talented engineer at NASA, Chris came up with the concept of mission control.

CAPCOM
Some astronauts work in mission control as CAPCOMs (capsule communicators). Their job is to communicate with astronauts in space. In this photo, Apollo 16 astronaut Charlie Duke is CAPCOM.

Flight Director
The most important person at mission control is the Flight Director, who is in charge of the current mission. This photo is of Gene Kranz, who was a Flight Director during Apollo 11.

Observation area
Special guests could watch what was happening from behind glass.

Mission control key

1. Booster Systems Engineer
2. Retrofire Officer
3. Flight Dynamics Officer
4. Guidance Officer
5. Flight Surgeon
6. CAPCOM
7. CSM and LM systems
8. Operations and Procedures Officer
9. Flight Director
10. Flight Activities Officer
11. Network Controller
12. Public Affairs Officer
13. Director of Flight Operations
14. Mission Director from NASA Headquarters
15. Department of Defence Representative
16. Special guests

Trailblazers

NASA

Katherine Johnson

Mathematician Katherine began her career working as a "human computer". She was personally requested by astronaut John Glenn to check calculations before his spaceflight, and she later received the Presidential Medal of Freedom.

NASA

Nancy Roman

With a PhD in astronomy, Nancy became NASA's first ever Chief of Astronomy, as well as the first woman to hold a senior position at NASA. Nancy did not let the fact that she was a woman stop her from having a career in the space industry.

NASA

Margaret Hamilton

A computer scientist and systems engineer, Margaret led the creation of the Apollo spacecraft's guidance and navigation systems. Her approach to software development was crucial to the success of Apollo. She later received the Presidential Medal of Freedom.

American women weren't allowed to be astronauts, but this didn't stop them from playing important roles during the space race.

In an era when women were expected to marry and stay at home, women at NASA were instead mathematicians, scientists, and engineers. Some faced additional unfair treatment in society because of the colour of their skin, but they were recognized by NASA for their abilities.

Some women worked as "human computers". They worked on maths problems and did complicated calculations by hand to understand how a spacecraft would behave during a mission. Today, computers

Melba Roy Mouton

NASA's Assistant Chief of Research Programs in the Trajectory and Geodynamics Division, Melba Roy led the "human computers" in their calculations. She had a masters in mathematics and later received awards for her service to the Apollo programme.

NASA

Billie Robertson

During the Apollo programme, Billie developed manuals for computer models of launches. A mathematician, she started her career working with rocket engines. She also worked on Wernher von Braun's team, developing guidance software for launches.

NASA

Annie Easley

Computer scientist Annie started her career as a "human computer" and later became a computer programmer. She developed and researched code to support many NASA programmes. Annie also earned a degree in mathematics while working full time.

are needed to do this work. Others helped to develop computer codes, which contributed to computer programs that we use in the world today.

These trailblazers worked hard to follow their passion for the space industry, turning ideas about space into reality. Their contributions were not only key to the USA's success during the space race, but for future missions too.

These women didn't set out to become role models, but their determination to help expand our knowledge of space, while facing the prejudice of the time, made them so. Although they were not as well known as the astronauts, this group, and many other women, were heroes in the space industry.

In order to get to the surface of the Moon, astronauts flew a special spacecraft called the Lunar Module (LM). It was extremely lightweight, and was carried into space inside the top of the Saturn V rocket.

Apollo 9

The first flight of the Lunar Module was actually around the Earth. It was tested by the crew of Apollo 9 in March 1969. Although it looks upside down in the photo, it isn't really because there is no up or down in space! The crew named the LM "Spider".

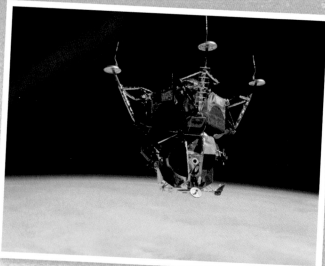

View of the Lunar Module from the Command Module

Radar
The radar antenna was used to measure distances when docking with the rest of the Apollo spacecraft.

Controls
The control panel was located inside the LM, where there were also small windows to help the astronauts find their landing sites.

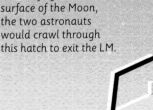

Forward hatch
Once safely on the surface of the Moon, the two astronauts would crawl through this hatch to exit the LM.

Ladder
The astronauts climbed down a ladder to get to the surface of the Moon.

Footpads
Surface contact sensor probes on the footpads told the commander when to switch the engine off after landing.

Overhead hatch
On its way to the Moon, the LM docked with the Command Module. The astronauts would then crawl through this hatch to get inside.

Thrusters
Thrusters helped the astronauts control the LM when flying in space.

Lift-off!

The Lunar Module was spilt into two parts: a descent stage and an ascent stage. When it was time to leave the Moon, the ascent stage's engine would fire, while the descent stage acted as a launch pad.

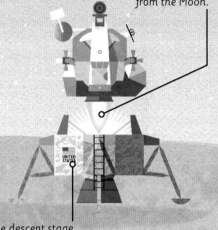

The ascent stage's engine fires to take the astronauts away from the Moon.

The descent stage remains on the surface of the Moon.

Astronauts
The LM was designed for two astronauts. To save weight, there were no seats. Instead, they had to fly it standing up.

Foil blankets
The LM was wrapped in a gold-coloured, foil-like skin. This acted as a heat blanket that protected the astronauts from extreme temperatures.

Descent engine
This engine was used to fly the LM to the surface of the Moon.

Legs
The LM had four landing legs. It was originally going to have just three, but there were fears that it could topple over.

Moon suit

On the Moon there is no air to breathe and no shelter from the extreme temperatures and the Sun's harmful rays. Astronauts need to wear a spacesuit to protect themselves and to be able to walk around safely on the surface.

Apollo spacesuit

The Apollo spacesuit was worn over other layers of protective clothing. It was designed to be worn not just on the Moon, but also during the launch to space and re-entry to Earth. The Portable Life Support System, protective boots and gloves, and a visor were added to the spacesuit when astronauts walked on the Moon.

Helmet and visor
Astronauts wore a clear bubble-shaped helmet with a visor over the top. The visor acted like a giant pair of sunglasses to protect the astronaut's eyes from the Sun.

Portable Life Support System (PLSS)
The PLSS – also known as "the backpack" – contained everything that astronauts needed to stay alive, including oxygen to breathe. It was also a power source for their communications system.

Remote Control Unit
Astronauts used this to communicate. It also provided live updates about the suit's condition and could be used to hold an astronaut's camera.

White outer layer
The outer layer was strong enough to prevent rips and tears, and keep astronauts protected from small meteorites.

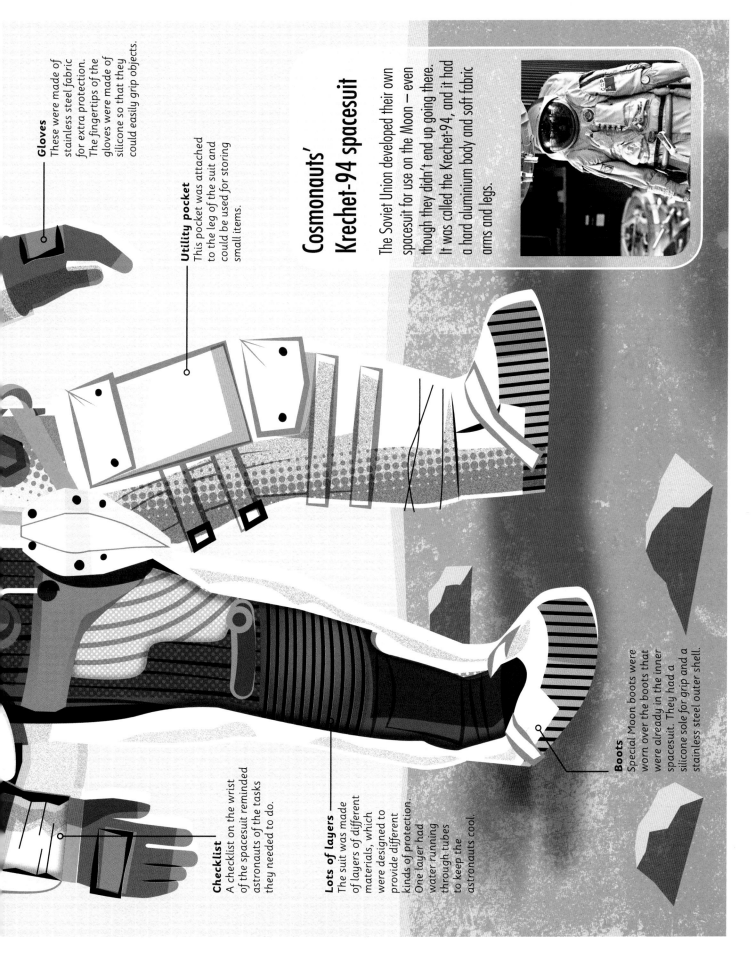

Gloves

These were made of stainless steel fabric for extra protection. The fingertips of the gloves were made of silicone so that they could easily grip objects.

Utility pocket

This pocket was attached to the leg of the suit and could be used for storing small items.

Cosmonauts' Krechet-94 spacesuit

The Soviet Union developed their own spacesuit for use on the Moon – even though they didn't end up going there. It was called the Krechet-94, and it had a hard aluminium body and soft fabric arms and legs.

Checklist

A checklist on the wrist of the spacesuit reminded astronauts of the tasks they needed to do.

Lots of layers

The suit was made of layers of different materials, which were designed to provide different kinds of protection. One layer had water running through tubes to keep the astronauts cool.

Boots

Special Moon boots were worn over the boots that were already in the inner spacesuit. They had a silicone sole for grip and a stainless steel outer shell.

Apollo 11

Michael Collins

Michael was a committed pilot and engineer, and as an astronaut he had already done two spacewalks. He was the Command Module pilot for Apollo 11, and he would orbit the Moon alone.

Neil Armstrong

Neil was the Commander of Apollo 11 and one of the greatest pilots that has ever lived. He was able to fly before he could drive, was cool-headed in dangerous situations, and had escaped death on several occasions.

Imagine being told that you are going to go on a mission to walk on the Moon. That is exactly what happened to Neil Armstrong and Buzz Aldrin. Along with Michael Collins, they made up the crew of Apollo 11. This was the first mission to attempt to land on the lunar surface – a place where no human had been before.

Apollo 11 mission patch
This patch was designed by the crew. The bald eagle is the national bird of the USA, and it is holding an olive branch to represent peace.

By now, NASA had mastered all of the skills needed for the mission. They had even flown the Lunar Module to within 15 km (9 miles) of the lunar surface, during Apollo 10, in preparation for a landing. Now, the hopes of achieving President Kennedy's goal and beating the Soviet Union rested with these three astronauts.

However, the Apollo 11 mission also had its dangers. There was a chance the astronauts might not make it home, and some scientists even thought that there was so much dust on the Moon's surface that the Lunar Module would sink. Ahead of the mission, the crew spent hundreds of hours practising in simulators and rehearsing every possible situation.

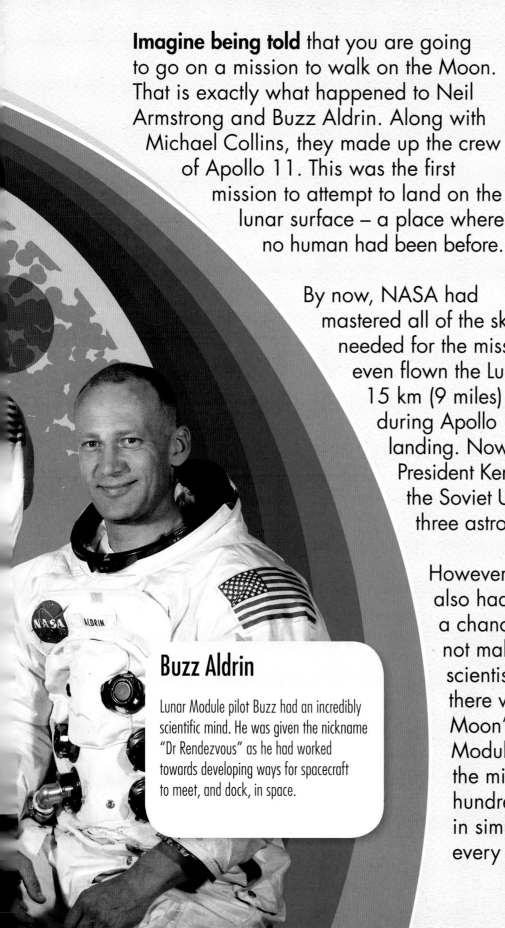

Buzz Aldrin

Lunar Module pilot Buzz had an incredibly scientific mind. He was given the nickname "Dr Rendezvous" as he had worked towards developing ways for spacecraft to meet, and dock, in space.

Suiting up

If you're going to be first to the Moon, you have to get up early! On 16 July 1969, the crew of Apollo 11 were woken up at 4:15 am. It was the day they were going to launch into space.

After eating breakfast, they had electrodes placed on their bodies. These were designed to provide information about the astronauts' breathing and heart rates during the mission. The crew were then helped into their spacesuits by technicians, which took just over an hour.

5:35 am

Neil prepares to put on his helmet during "suit-up".

4:45 am

The crew eat a breakfast of steak and eggs, and were joined by the head of the astronaut office, Deke Slayton (right).

6:48 am

Neil leads the crew across the walkway to board the Apollo spacecraft.

6:27 am

The astronauts wave goodbye to NASA staff as they walk to the Astrovan.

Once snug inside their spacesuits, Neil, Michael, and Buzz had to carry their air supply with them. They waved goodbye to NASA staff and waiting reporters and boarded a van (called the Astrovan), which would take them to the launch pad.

At the launch pad, they rode in a lift, then crossed a walkway before being helped into their spacecraft by technicians. The spacecraft hatch then shut with a clang – the countdown to the Moon had begun.

Lift-off!

More than two hours after the astronauts had boarded the Saturn V, the launch teams completed their final checks. The rocket started to come to life and the final countdown began: "10, 9 – ignition sequence starts – 6, 5, 4, 3, 2, 1, 0. All engines running. Lift-off. We have a lift-off". The rocket roared as it began to rise. The noise was so great that it reached spectators watching from more than 5 km (3 miles) away.

This was the fourth time that the Saturn V rocket had ever flown with people inside it. However, for the

first time in history, and before the Soviet Union, the American Apollo 11 crew would attempt to walk on the surface of another world.

Thousands of people had made the journey to Florida, USA, to watch the launch. There were so many photographers taking pictures that the sound of cameras clicking began to drown out the noise of the rocket. The Saturn V rose up through the sky as people looked up in disbelief. In Launch Control, Wernher von Braun watched the rocket he had created as it started its journey to the Moon.

Journey to the Moon

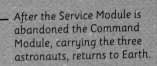

After the Service Module is abandoned the Command Module, carrying the three astronauts, returns to Earth.

The Saturn V rocket launches into space.

The Command/Service Module, named Columbia, separates from the rocket and the Lunar Module. It then turns around and docks back with the Lunar Module.

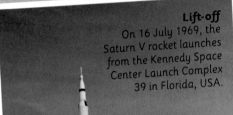

Lift-off
On 16 July 1969, the Saturn V rocket launches from the Kennedy Space Center Launch Complex 39 in Florida, USA.

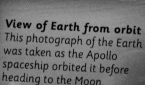

View of Earth from orbit
This photograph of the Earth was taken as the Apollo spaceship orbited it before heading to the Moon.

From launch to splashdown, the Apollo 11 mission would last eight days. After leaving Earth's orbit, Neil, Buzz, and Michael were in constant communication with the team at Mission Control. They even appeared on TV to talk about their journey.

Goodbye Earth
As they continued on their journey, the astronauts looked out of the window to see Earth becoming smaller and smaller.

Lunar Module
Command Module pilot Michael Collins took this photograph of the Lunar Module.

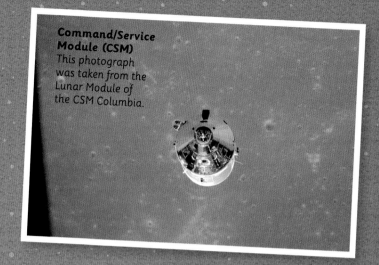

Command/Service Module (CSM)
This photograph was taken from the Lunar Module of the CSM Columbia.

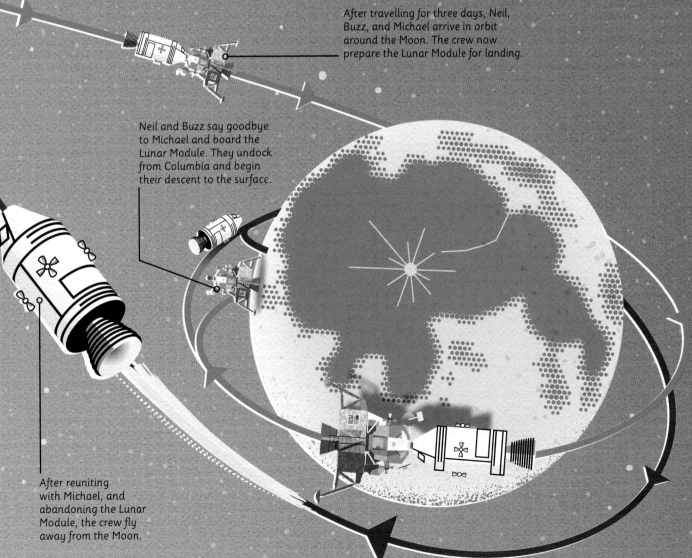

After travelling for three days, Neil, Buzz, and Michael arrive in orbit around the Moon. The crew now prepare the Lunar Module for landing.

Neil and Buzz say goodbye to Michael and board the Lunar Module. They undock from Columbia and begin their descent to the surface.

After reuniting with Michael, and abandoning the Lunar Module, the crew fly away from the Moon.

The Eagle has landed

Once in orbit around the Moon, Neil and Buzz said goodbye to Michael and crawled inside the Lunar Module, called "Eagle", to begin their descent to the surface. However, the journey was not without danger.

On the way down, the mission nearly had to be aborted after an alarm sounded just minutes into the landing sequence. Back at Mission Control in Houston, the team worked hard and managed to solve the problem.

As they continued towards the surface, Buzz concentrated on the instrument panel, calling out critical information, as Neil steered. But there was another problem – they were heading for a boulder field! Neil began to look for a new place to land.

With less than 30 seconds of fuel remaining, the descent engine began to kick up dust as the Eagle closed in on the surface. Then, touchdown. Neil radioed back to Earth the famous lines: "Houston, Tranquility Base here, the Eagle has landed". The date was 20 July 1969.

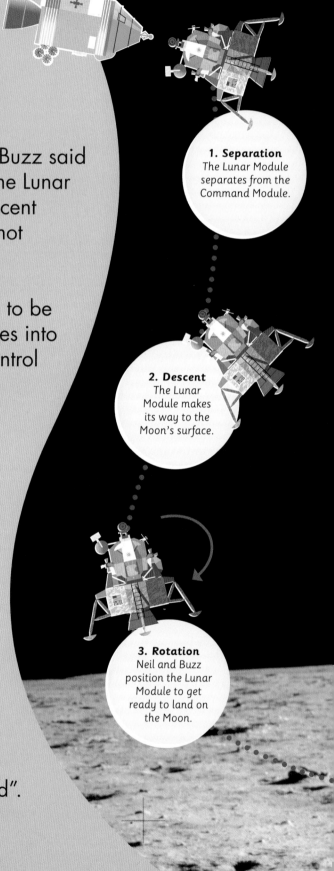

1. Separation
The Lunar Module separates from the Command Module.

2. Descent
The Lunar Module makes its way to the Moon's surface.

3. Rotation
Neil and Buzz position the Lunar Module to get ready to land on the Moon.

4. Landing
The astronauts land safely on an area of the Moon called the Sea of Tranquility.

The Eagle on the surface of the Moon, photographed by Neil. Buzz can be seen climbing down the ladder.

USA

Among those watching in the USA were the families of the crew. Michael Collins's wife, Pat (far left), is seen here with their daughter, Ann, who is wearing a red dressing gown.

Japan

The world watches

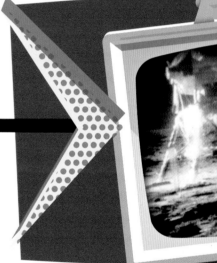

UK

In London, crowds gathered in front of a huge TV screen that was put up in Trafalgar Square.

In Tokyo, this family are sitting around their TV set as Neil and Buzz are seen saluting from the Moon.

Pope Paul VI watched the TV coverage as Neil and Buzz landed safely on the Moon.

Italy

More than 600 million people were watching as Neil Armstrong climbed down the ladder of the Lunar Module and stepped onto the Moon. As he did so, he uttered the words, "It's one small step for man, one giant leap for mankind".

News reporters who were covering the story watched with wonder. Neil Armstrong, a 38-year-old American, had just become the first person to set foot on the surface of the Moon. Something that had seemed impossible for so long was actually happening.

In Kuwait, families sat down together to watch the footage on TV.

Kuwait

Australia

At Mascot Airport, Sydney, people stopped what they were doing and watched Neil take his first steps on the Moon.

American flag
Neil and Buzz planted an American flag on the Moon. They also left a plaque that read: "We came in peace for all mankind".

Buzz's footprint
This is a photograph of Buzz's bootprint on the surface of the Moon. It was one of the first footprints on another world.

Experiments
The astronauts did experiments on the surface of the Moon. This one was designed to study charged particles from the Sun called solar wind.

On the Moon

Shortly after Neil set foot on the Moon, Buzz joined him on the surface, describing what he saw as "magnificent desolation". The Moon had an empty, grey landscape, no air, and a black sky. Neil and Buzz were the only living things there.

On the Moon, there is less gravity than on Earth. This means that the astronauts could bounce around on the surface, even though they were wearing heavy spacesuits. The two astronauts gathered rock samples to bring back for scientists to study,

as well as setting up experiments. They even spoke to the President of the United States, Richard Nixon, who congratulated them. He told Neil and Buzz that it was "the most historic phone call that had ever been made from the White House".

After 2 hours and 31 minutes, the astronauts' moonwalk was over. Neil and Buzz climbed back up the ladder into the safety of the Lunar Module. They rested and prepared to reunite with Michael in the Command Module to return home.

Back inside
Buzz took this photo of Neil inside the Lunar Module after they had completed their moonwalk.

Buzz Aldrin on the Moon
Neil took this photo of Buzz on the Moon. You can see Neil reflected in Buzz's visor. There are hardly any pictures of Neil on the Moon as he was holding their only camera most of the time.

The Apollo 11 astronauts' journey home from the Moon was not without danger. In fact, if it wasn't for a felt-tip pen, Neil and Buzz might never have left the surface of the Moon. Buzz had to use the pen to push a switch to start the engine of the Lunar Module, Eagle, after the switch had accidentally been broken off!

to Earth. Just before re-entry into Earth's atmosphere, Neil, Buzz, and Michael strapped themselves tightly in their seats.

The return through the atmosphere was like being inside a fireball. As the Command Module passed through the atmosphere at high speed, the air in front of the module was squashed, which created extreme heat. However, a heat shield protected the module and the astronauts inside.

Splashdown!

After rejoining Michael, they fired the engine of the Command/Service Module, Columbia, and began their voyage back

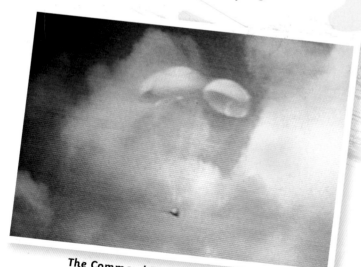

The Command Module falls to Earth

At about 3 km (2 miles) from the ground, the main parachutes fired open. They helped to slow the Command Module down. Then, splashdown! The module landed in the Pacific Ocean. The crew were home.

At Mission Control, there were celebrations. The Americans had won the race to the Moon.

Quarantine

After their return from the Moon, Neil, Buzz, and Michael had to spend 21 days in quarantine, or isolation. There had been fears that they may have been carrying deadly lunar germs! It was later confirmed, however, that the Moon is lifeless, so there was no need for concern.

Inside the Mobile Quarantine Facility

The crew meets US President Richard Nixon

Astronauts on tour

After Apollo 11, astronauts Neil, Buzz, and Michael became some of the most famous people on the planet. Everyone wanted to meet the people who had been to the Moon.

Once out of quarantine, the Apollo 11 astronauts travelled through American cities for parades, before embarking on a tour around the world with their wives: Janet Armstrong, Joan Aldrin, and Pat Collins.

After being the first nation to successfully land people on the Moon, the USA wanted to share its knowledge about space travel with other nations. In 45 days the group visited 24 different countries, meeting royalty and politicians and shaking hands with thousands of people. This tour was officially known as the Giantstep-Apollo 11 Presidential Goodwill Tour.

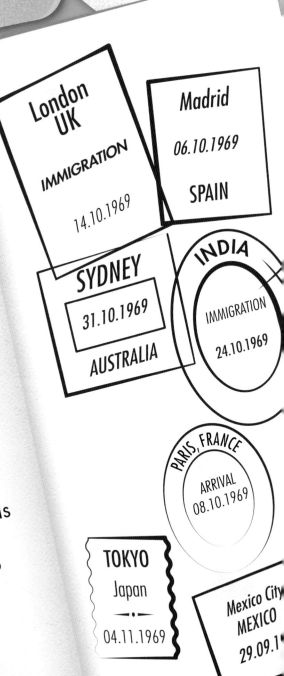

London UK
IMMIGRATION
14.10.1969

Madrid
06.10.1969
SPAIN

SYDNEY
31.10.1969
AUSTRALIA

INDIA
IMMIGRATION
24.10.1969

PARIS, FRANCE
ARRIVAL
08.10.1969

TOKYO
Japan
04.11.1969

Mexico City
MEXICO
29.09.1

Mexico City, Mexico
The astronauts were swamped by a crowd of thousands in Mexico City. They are wearing sombrero hats and poncho capes.

JFK
LHR
PA 0102
TRANSFER

Paris, France
The astronauts were presented with solid gold replicas of the Lunar Module in France, paid for by readers of the French newspaper Le Figaro.

London, UK
The group travelled to Buckingham Palace to meet Queen Elizabeth II and the rest of the British royal family.

Madrid, Spain
At the Royal Palace of El Pardo, the group met with General Francisco Franco. He was the ruler of Spain from 1939 until 1975.

Tokyo, Japan
The astronauts waved to crowds from the front of their motorcade in Tokyo. They had only recently arrived from South Korea.

RATION

Bombay, India
Neil, Buzz, and Michael led a parade through the streets of Bombay – now called Mumbai.

Sydney, Australia
The astronauts attended a welcome reception in Hyde Park, Sydney, before giving speeches about what it was like to go to the Moon.

A successful failure

FOR JIM LOVELL (LEFT), HIS NEW MISSION WAS VERY SPECIAL. HE'D ALREADY GONE AROUND THE MOON WITH APOLLO 8. NOW HE'D RETURN TO WALK ON IT AS COMMANDER OF APOLLO 13, WITH JACK SWIGERT (CENTRE) AND FRED HAISE (RIGHT).

"LIFT-OFF!"

ON 11 APRIL 1970, THEY BEGAN THEIR VOYAGE. IT WOULD BE NASA'S THIRD ATTEMPT TO SEND PEOPLE TO THE LUNAR SURFACE. HOWEVER, THE PUBLIC HAD STARTED TO BECOME BORED WITH SEEING PEOPLE ON THE MOON!

"HOUSTON, WE'VE **HAD** A PROBLEM."

ON 13 APRIL, AFTER SWITCHING ON THE FANS THAT STIR THE OXYGEN AND HYDROGEN TANKS IN THE SERVICE MODULE, THE ASTRONAUTS HEARD A BANG. THEY WERE IN SERIOUS TROUBLE. THE OXYGEN TANK HAD EXPLODED AND THE SERVICE MODULE WAS DAMAGED. MISSION CONTROL IN HOUSTON, TEXAS, ORDERED THEM HOME.

THE ASTRONAUTS FACED A NUMBER OF TECHNICAL PROBLEMS, SUCH AS A BUILD-UP OF TOXIC CARBON DIOXIDE IN THE LM. HOWEVER, WITH THE HELP OF THE TEAM BACK ON EARTH, THEY WERE ABLE TO FIND SOLUTIONS.

WITH LIMITED POWER, THE CREW'S BEST HOPE FOR SURVIVAL WAS TO USE THE LUNAR MODULE (LM) AS A LIFE RAFT. THEY CONTINUED TO THE MOON AND CIRCLED IT TO "SLINGSHOT" THE SPACECRAFT BACK TO EARTH.

THE CREW MOVED BACK INTO THE COMMAND MODULE AND PREPARED FOR RE-ENTRY AFTER DUMPING THE LM. AROUND THE WORLD, PEOPLE WATCHED AND HELD THEIR BREATH.

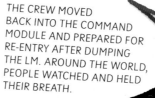

AS APOLLO 13 NEARED EARTH, THE CREW DISCARDED THE SERVICE MODULE. OUTSIDE, THEY COULD SEE THAT AN ENTIRE SIDE PANEL HAD BEEN BLOWN OFF.

SPLASHDOWN!

AFTER DAYS OF NONSTOP WORK, THE TEAM AT MISSION CONTROL HAD SUCCEEDED IN BRINGING THE ASTRONAUTS HOME. THE ROOM ERUPTED WITH CHEERS AND CLAPPING.

THE CREW MET WITH PRESIDENT NIXON AND WERE AWARDED THE PRESIDENTIAL MEDAL OF FREEDOM. SOMETIMES YOU DON'T ALWAYS HAVE TO SUCCEED TO BE SUCCESSFUL!

We don't have personal jetpacks yet, but during the space race they were being designed and tested. On 20 April 1961 – not long after Yuri Gagarin became the first person to travel to space – the jetpack was flown for the first time. It was unveiled at Niagara Falls, on the border between the United States and Canada, and testing continued over the coming decades.

The race to the Moon made people think that anything was possible, and the idea of having a personal jetpack did not seem too crazy. The jetpack, officially known as a rocket belt, was invented by Wendell Moore, an American engineer at Bell Aerosystems. He had helped to create all types of other flying devices, such as a flying chair and a two-person flying pogo stick.

One of the people who got to fly Wendell's inventions was Bill Suitor. He had known Wendell since he was a teenager, when he'd mowed his lawn. There had been hope that some of Wendell's inventions, such as the two-person pogo stick, could be used to help astronauts move around on the surface of the Moon.

Jetpacks and pogo sticks

"When you're 19, *flying a jetpack* doesn't seem **too scary**. Now that I am older and look back, I realize **how frightening** it could be."
— **Bill Suitor**

Rocket belt
This photograph is of
Bill Suitor testing a
jetpack in 1966.

During the first three lunar landings, astronauts could only walk on the surface of the Moon. Starting with Apollo 15, a car was sent with the astronauts to the Moon, which allowed them to travel for kilometres at a time.

Lunar Roving Vehicle

Known as the Lunar Rover, or LRV, this battery-powered car travelled as fast as 18 kph (11 mph). It could transport two astronauts, their equipment, and lunar samples.

Astronaut
Riding on the LRV was bumpy so the astronauts had to wear seatbelts that were fastened using Velcro™.

Wheels
Titanium treads helped the wheels grip the rough lunar soil.

Hand control
The astronaut could steer the LRV using a T-shaped hand control.

"You really can't **get lost** on the Moon: **just follow your tracks back!**"
– Charlie Duke, Apollo 16

Antenna
This large antenna was used to communicate with the team back on Earth.

Television camera
This camera filmed the Moon in colour and could be controlled by people back on Earth.

On the Moon

Jim Irwin and Dave Scott – the landing crew of Apollo 15 – were the first people to drive on the Moon. In this photograph, Jim salutes the American flag. The LRV is on the right.

Apollo 15 landing site

Unpacking the rover

Getting a car to the Moon is incredibly difficult. The LRV, which weighed 210 kg (462 lb), was folded up in a special compartment and unpacked by the astronauts once they were on the Moon.

Lowering
The astronaut lowers the LRV from the storage bay at the bottom of the Lunar Module (LM) by pulling down on straps.

Chassis unfolds
As the LRV is lowered, the frame of the rover (called the chassis) and wheels unfold.

LRV disconnects
Once the chassis is unfolded, the LRV is disconnected from the LM. Then the seats and footrest are unfolded.

Three astronauts travelled to the Moon in each Apollo mission, but only two of them would walk on its surface. The other astronaut – known as the Command Module Pilot – had to remain orbiting the Moon, all alone.

The role of the Command Module Pilot was very important. They had to look after the Command/Service Module (CSM), which was the crew's only way to get back to Earth, and to study the Moon from above. In the event of a catastrophic failure on the Moon, they would have to return to Earth alone, although fortunately this never happened. In the later Apollo missions, the Command Module Pilot even got to perform a spacewalk to fetch camera film that had been on the outside of their spacecraft.

As the CSM passed around the far side of the Moon, its pilot would be completely cut off from all communications. This made the Command Module Pilots completely isolated. However, they didn't have time to feel lonely as they were kept busy with tasks to complete before they met up with the other astronauts. In the blackness of space, they could also look out into the Universe and see more stars than they could ever count.

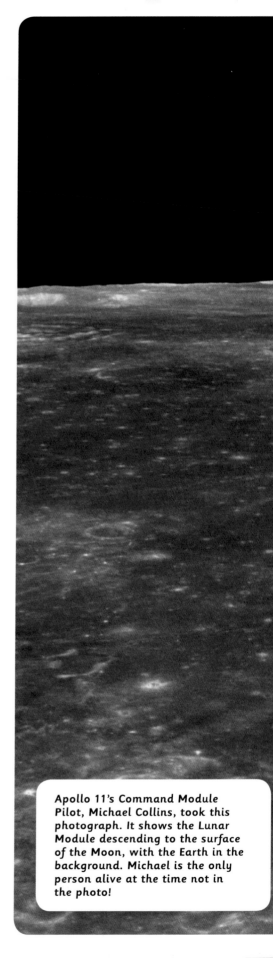

Apollo 11's Command Module Pilot, Michael Collins, took this photograph. It shows the Lunar Module descending to the surface of the Moon, with the Earth in the background. Michael is the only person alive at the time not in the photo!

What did Command Module Pilots do?

OPERATIONS CHECKLIST

1. Know all the systems on the Command/Service Module (CSM)	✔
2. Serve as flight engineer during the launch	✔
3. Navigate and perform course corrections on the journey	✔
4. Pilot the CSM while orbiting the Moon	✔
5. Photograph the surface of the Moon from the CSM	✔
6. Look for landing sites for future Apollo missions	✔
7. Rescue the Lunar Module if it cannot dock in space	✔

ALARM CODES

NAVIGATION

LANDING DATA

RE-ENTRY DATA

The last mission

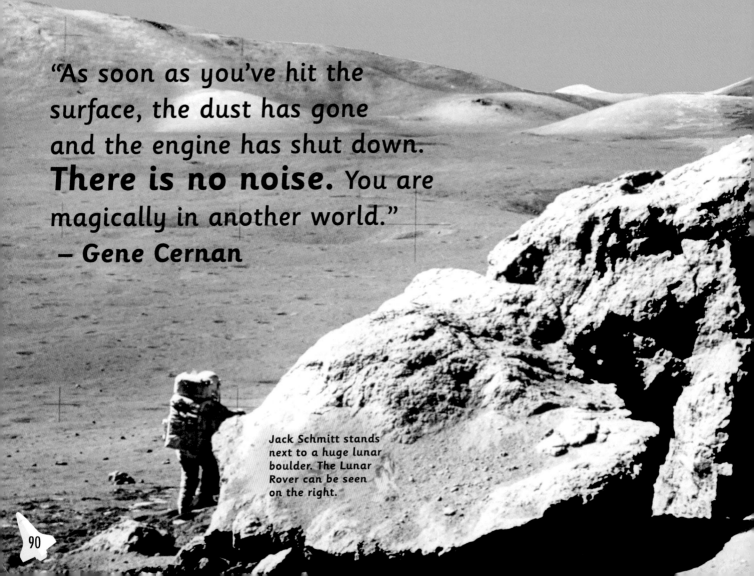

In December 1972, Apollo 17 was the last mission to the Moon. Originally, 10 Moon landings had been planned. However, due to cuts in funding, only six went ahead.

For Commander Eugene "Gene" Cernan, being in charge of the final mission was the proudest moment of his life. He was joined by Lunar Module Pilot Harrison "Jack" Schmitt, the only scientist to visit the Moon, and Command Module Pilot Ronald Evans.

Apollo 17 spent three days on the Moon exploring a valley called Taurus-Littrow, where they discovered orange soil. Later, scientists would

"As soon as you've hit the surface, the dust has gone and the engine has shut down. **There is no noise.** *You are magically in another world."*
– Gene Cernan

Jack Schmitt stands next to a huge lunar boulder. The Lunar Rover can be seen on the right.

find very tiny amounts of water in the samples bought back to Earth, helping them to understand more about how the Moon formed.

Before leaving the Moon, Gene Cernan looked back at his footprints in the soil. He knew he would never visit again. The Apollo missions to the Moon were over.

Last visitors
Gene (left) and Jack (right) are still the last two people to have visited the Moon.

Lunar soil
The orange soil discovered on the final Apollo mission got its unusual colour from ancient volcanic activity.

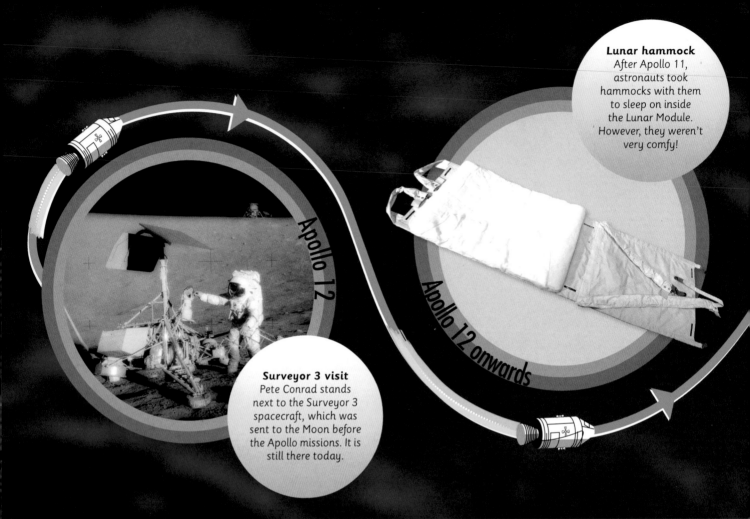

Apollo 12

Lunar hammock
After Apollo 11, astronauts took hammocks with them to sleep on inside the Lunar Module. However, they weren't very comfy!

Apollo 12 onwards

Surveyor 3 visit
Pete Conrad stands next to the Surveyor 3 spacecraft, which was sent to the Moon before the Apollo missions. It is still there today.

Apollo's legacy

The Apollo missions changed the way we saw the Moon forever. In total, astronauts brought back 382 kg (842 lb) of lunar rocks, pebbles, and dust. These samples are still being studied by scientists to this day. They have helped us understand more about the history of the Moon, but also more about the Earth. For example, most scientists now think that the Moon was formed when a young Earth was struck by a Mars-sized object.

Soil samples collected by the Apollo astronauts have also helped scientists learn more about the Sun's activity over many millions of years. This is because the Moon doesn't have a protective atmosphere to block the Sun's stronger rays, like Earth does, so we can see how these rays have left their mark on lunar rocks.

Golf on the Moon
This grainy video image shows Apollo 14's Alan Shepard playing golf on the Moon. He never got his golf ball back!

Apollo 14

Apollo 14

Memorial on the Moon
A model of a fallen astronaut beside a plaque honours those who lost their lives in the space race.

Apollo 15

Moon trees
Hundreds of tree seeds were taken on board Apollo 14 by Command Module Pilot Stuart Roosa. They were later planted back on Earth and grew into "Moon trees".

The findings are pieces in a jigsaw puzzle as we try to piece together our understanding of not only the Earth and the Solar System, but also the Universe around us. We are only just beginning to scratch the surface of what is to come, but Apollo has given us a great start.

However, Apollo was as much about people as it was about science. When future explorers return and visit the landing sites, they will find all sorts of treasures. They will read plaques detailing how people "came in peace for all mankind", find the lunar rovers that astronauts enjoyed driving on the surface, and they might even find Alan Shepard's missing golf ball! To this day, Apollo is the greatest story in human exploration.

Footprints on the Moon

Out of every human that has ever existed, only 12 have walked on the Moon.

Landing site map
This is a photograph of the Apollo 17 landing site, taken by NASA's Lunar Reconnaissance Orbiter (LRO) in 2011. You can see footprints, tyre tracks, and the descent stage of the Lunar Module.

Apollo 11
Neil Armstrong

After Apollo 11, Neil became a household name. However, he avoided the spotlight and returned to his passion — flying planes!

Apollo 11
Buzz Aldrin

After the Moon, Buzz's next goal was to help humans get to Mars. He travelled the world inspiring others about the Red Planet.

Apollo 12
Charles "Pete" Conrad

Pete's first words on the Moon were: "Whoopie! Man, that may have been a small one for Neil, but that's a long one for me."

Astronauts' footprints

Descent stage of Lunar Module

Apollo 12
Alan Bean

After walking on the Moon, Alan became a painter, inspiring others with his lunar landscapes.

Apollo 14
Alan Shepard

Alan was the only one of the Mercury 7 to walk on the Moon. While there, he hit a golf ball, which he said travelled for "miles and miles".

Apollo 14
Edgar Mitchell

When he returned from the Apollo 14 mission, Edgar helped found the Association of Space Explorers — to be a member you have to have gone to space!

Tyre tracks

Apollo 15 — Dave Scott

During an Apollo 15 moonwalk with Jim Irwin, Dave discovered a Moon rock that was four billion years old!

Apollo 15 — Jim Irwin

From the surface of the Moon, Jim looked back at Earth and described it as "beautiful and fragile".

Apollo 16 — John Young

One of NASA's greatest astronauts, John travelled to space a total of six times and was the first person to fly the Space Shuttle.

Apollo 16 — Charlie Duke

At 36 years old, Charlie was the youngest astronaut to walk on the Moon.

Family photo on the Moon

Charlie Duke left this photograph of his family on the Moon. Another astronaut, Gene Cernan, scratched his daughter's initials on the Moon's surface on a separate mission.

Apollo 17 — Eugene "Gene" Cernan

Gene was the last person to walk on the Moon. He dedicated his life to promoting space exploration, hoping that people would walk on the Moon again.

Apollo 17 — Harrison "Jack" Schmitt

Jack was the only scientist to walk on the Moon. After Apollo 17 he became a US Senator.

Quiet heroes

Chris Kraft
The concept of mission control was developed by Chris, who was an engineer at NASA. He became NASA's first Flight Director and NASA even named their mission control building after him.

Deke Slayton
One of the Mercury 7, Deke was originally unable to go to space due to a heart condition. Instead, he managed astronaut training and operations. He played a key role in selecting mission crews, including deciding who would be the first on the Moon. Thanks to advances in medical science, his dream of going to space came true in 1975 when he took part in the Apollo-Soyuz mission.

Astronauts may have been the public face of Apollo, but behind them was a team of about 400,000 people.

There were the women who hand-stitched every spacesuit, the janitors who made sure the spacecraft were clean, and the scientists and engineers who worked hard to solve seemingly impossible problems to put rockets into space. Every single job mattered, and everyone had to do their part to make sure that the Apollo missions were successful.

Scientists and engineers from all around the world helped during the Apollo missions. And countries

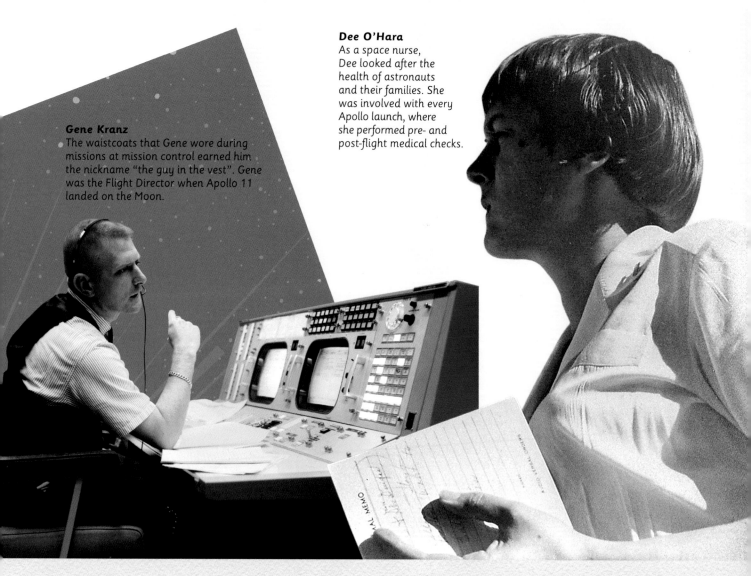

Gene Kranz
The waistcoats that Gene wore during missions at mission control earned him the nickname "the guy in the vest". Gene was the Flight Director when Apollo 11 landed on the Moon.

Dee O'Hara
As a space nurse, Dee looked after the health of astronauts and their families. She was involved with every Apollo launch, where she performed pre- and post-flight medical checks.

as far and wide as Australia, the United Kingdom, and Spain helped to track every Apollo spacecraft on its journey.

There are too many quiet heroes to name. One of the greatest lessons to come from the space race and Apollo is that when a group of experts work together as a team, they can achieve more than if they work alone.

While the astronauts who walked on the Moon were able to look up and say "I went there", thousands of other people were able to look at the Moon in a different way, knowing that they helped to send people there.

Peace in space

On 17 July 1975, an American Apollo spacecraft and a Soviet Soyuz spacecraft joined together in space. After they docked, the commanders of each crew floated through the connecting hatch and shook hands. This moment was watched by millions of people on Earth, as the docking marked the end of the space race between the USA and the Soviet Union. These competing nations could now work together to explore space.

The mission was made up of two crews – Soviet cosmonauts Alexei Leonov and Valery Kubasov, and American astronauts Thomas Stafford, Deke Slayton, and Vance Brand. They took phone calls from both American President Gerald Ford and Soviet leader Leonid Brezhnev. The crews also performed science experiments together and exchanged gifts.

The group assembled a plaque to mark their joint mission, with one side made in the USA and the other from the Soviet Union. After two days together, the crews said their goodbyes, undocked, and set off on separate space missions before returning home.

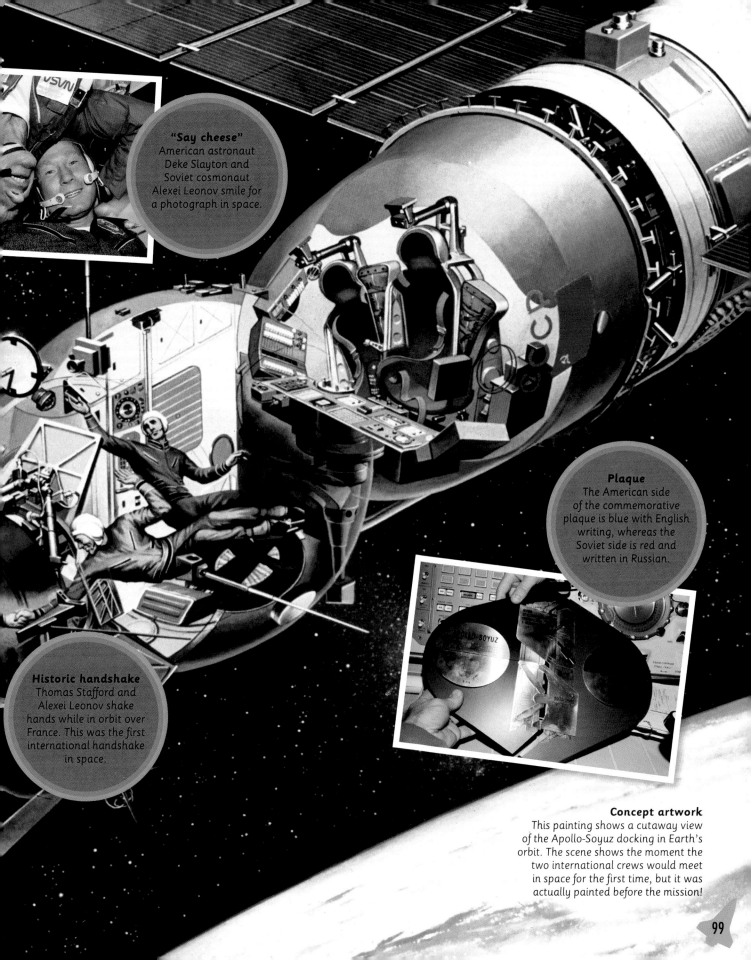

"Say cheese"
American astronaut Deke Slayton and Soviet cosmonaut Alexei Leonov smile for a photograph in space.

Plaque
The American side of the commemorative plaque is blue with English writing, whereas the Soviet side is red and written in Russian.

Historic handshake
Thomas Stafford and Alexei Leonov shake hands while in orbit over France. This was the first international handshake in space.

Concept artwork
This painting shows a cutaway view of the Apollo-Soyuz docking in Earth's orbit. The scene shows the moment the two international crews would meet in space for the first time, but it was actually painted before the mission!

What the Soviets did next

Many people thought the Soviet Union would be first to send people to the Moon. They'd had many successes in space – they sent the first spacecraft to the Moon and, later, were the first to photograph the far side of the Moon. In September 1968, they even sent tortoises around the Moon, before returning them safely to Earth.

However, the Soviets never succeeded in sending a crewed spacecraft to the Moon. Instead, following Apollo 11, they focused on robotic missions, which were cheaper to carry out.

They sent robotic spacecraft to other planets and were the first to send back photos from the surface of Venus. They also created the first space stations, designed for people to live and work in space.

Soviet lunar lander

The Soviets designed a lander to put a person on the Moon, but it was never used. Instead, they sent a robotic probe, called Luna 16, which returned to Earth with a sample of lunar soil.

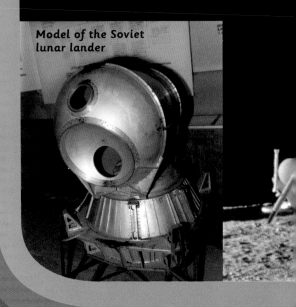

Model of the Soviet lunar lander

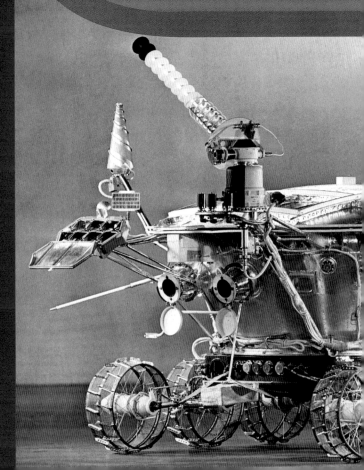

An artist's impression of Luna 16 on the surface of the Moon

Exploring Venus

The Soviets were initially more successful than the United States at exploring the planet Venus's surface. Between 1970 and 1985 they landed several spacecraft there, including the Venera spacecraft, as celebrated on this stamp. The Venera spacecraft sent back photographs from the surface.

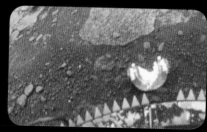

Colour photo of Venus's surface, taken by Venera 13 in 1982

Soviet rover

Lunokhod 1 was a robotic rover that was 2.3 m (7½ ft) long and 1.5 m (5 ft) tall. It explored the surface of the Moon for 10 months in 1970–1971.

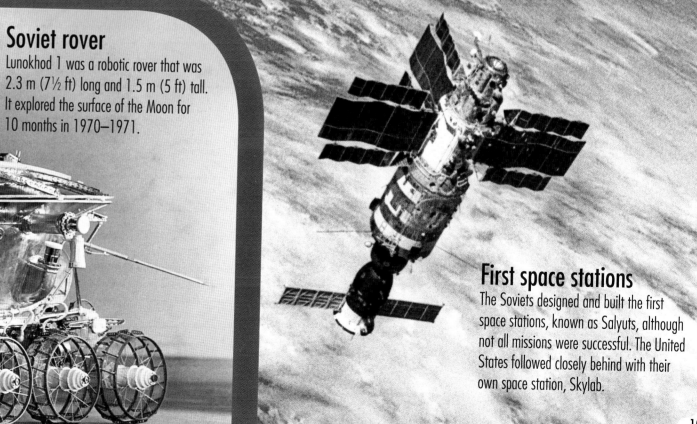

First space stations

The Soviets designed and built the first space stations, known as Salyuts, although not all missions were successful. The United States followed closely behind with their own space station, Skylab.

101

The Voyager missions

Our curiosity about space did not end with the Apollo programme. In fact, Apollo was just the beginning of our space adventure. In 1977, NASA launched twin robotic spacecraft called Voyager 1 and Voyager 2. They were sent on a journey across our Solar System to explore the outer planets. They travelled to places no human-made object had ever been to before, and are still on their journey to this day!

Spacecraft
The Voyager spacecraft were designed so that they could send messages back to Earth from beyond our Solar System.

Launch
Voyager 1 lifts off from Cape Canaveral, Florida, USA. It is named Voyager 1 because it would be the first spacecraft to reach Jupiter and Saturn.

Jupiter
Voyager 1 reaches Jupiter. It takes images that reveal that Jupiter's Great Red Spot is actually a huge storm. It also discovers volcanoes on Jupiter's moon, Io.

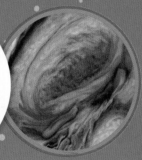

5 September 1977

5 March 1979

9 November 1980

Voyager 1

Voyager 2

20 August 1977

9 July 1979

25 August 1981

Launch
Voyager 2 launches into space from Cape Canaveral. It launched before Voyager 1, but it is named Voyager 2 as it would reach Jupiter and Saturn after Voyager 1.

Jupiter
Voyager 2 takes images of Jupiter's ring system and observes volcanic eruptions on Jupiter's moon, Io.

Saturn
Voyager 2 has its closest encounter with Saturn. It photographs the planet and flies by some of its icy moons, including Tethys and Iapetus.

The Golden Record

If aliens ever discover one of the Voyager spacecraft, they will find a Golden Record. This record contains sounds and greetings from Earth, showing what life is like here. It's a bit like the cosmic equivalent of a message in a bottle!

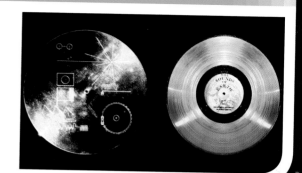

Saturn
Voyager 1 photographs Saturn and its largest moon, Titan. The spacecraft also discovers three new moons around the planet: Atlas, Pandora, and Prometheus.

Earth
Six billion km (3.7 billion miles) away from the Sun, Voyager 1 takes a photograph of Earth, which looks like a tiny pale blue dot.

Beyond our Solar System
Voyager 1 becomes the first human-made object to leave the Solar System.

14 February 1990

25 August 2012

24 January 1986

25 August 1989

Uranus
Voyager 2 becomes the first and only spacecraft to visit Uranus. Images taken by the spacecraft reveal what the planet looks like up-close.

Neptune
At Neptune, Voyager 2 discovers six new moons and a giant storm on the planet, nicknamed "The Great Dark Spot".

The start of the 1980s saw a new type of mission for NASA astronauts – leaving Earth using the Space Shuttle. While earlier spacecraft could only be used once, the Space Shuttle was designed for many flights.

Rudder
The rudder was used to help slow the Orbiter down before landing.

Fuel tanks
Fuel for the main engines was stored in two tanks.

Space Shuttle Main Engines (SSME)
Three main engines helped to push the Shuttle into orbit and steer it in the right direction.

Lift-off!
The Space Shuttle came in three parts: the Orbiter, which housed the astronauts; a large orange fuel tank called the External Tank; and two Solid Rocket Boosters, which blasted the Shuttle into space.

Heat shield
Tiles on the edge of the wings and the underside of the Orbiter protected it from extreme heat during re-entry.

Spacewalking
Astronauts could go outside through an airlock to perform spacewalks.

Canadarm
The Canadarm was a robotic arm that astronauts could use to release and capture satellites.

SOVIET SHUTTLE

The Soviet Union built its own version of the Space Shuttle called the Buran. However, it made just one flight, which was uncrewed, in 1988.

Landing

Although the Space Shuttle orbited the Earth upside down, it would flip around just before it re-entered the atmosphere so its heat shield could protect it. It landed by gliding down onto a runway. To help it slow down, a parachute opened up behind the Orbiter.

Cargo bay
Satellites and parts of the International Space Station were transported in the cargo bay.

Canada

Discovery

Cockpit
During launch and re-entry, the commander and pilot would sit at the front of the cockpit.

Mid-deck
This area contained lockers, extra seats for astronauts, a galley to prepare food, and a door to the airlock.

Payload bay doors
Two hinged doors could be opened during orbit to deploy satellites. The open doors also helped cool the Orbiter.

Landing gear
Wheels under the nose and the wings were deployed for landing on the runway.

Shannon Lucid

Rhea Seddon

Kathryn Sullivan

Judith Resnik

Anna Fisher

Sally Ride

First female astronaut group

In 1978, NASA recruited their first female astronauts. On 18 June 1983, Sally Ride became the first American woman in space.

A new generation

The Space Shuttle era paved the way for a new generation of NASA astronauts. In the past, all of the astronauts had been men, and most were military test pilots. However, society was changing and becoming more inclusive, and there were now more opportunities for African-Americans, like Guion Bluford, to go to space.

For the first time, NASA recruited women with the intention of sending them to space. Among them was Judith Resnik, who had trained as an electrical engineer. The first female astronauts were selected in 1978, and they helped to inspire more women to go to space.

Space also started to become more global. More countries wanted to be involved so that they could benefit from new discoveries in science and technology. Although the Soviet Union and the USA were still the only nations that could send people to space, both would fly astronauts from other countries, such as Saudi Arabia, the United Kingdom, and India.

First African-American in space

On 30 August 1983, Guion Bluford – an engineer and fighter pilot – became the first African-American to travel to space.

First female Space Shuttle Commander

On 23 July 1999, Eileen Collins became the first female to command a space mission.

International astronauts

People from all over the world started to travel to space. After returning from their missions, they promoted space travel and its benefits in their home nations.

Sultan Salman Abdulaziz Al-Saud, Saudi Arabia

Helen Sharman, United Kingdom

Rakesh Sharma, India

Mir

The Soviet Union began construction on the space station Mir in 1986. Meaning "peace" in Russian, Mir was assembled in space over a period of 10 years. In its day, it was the largest human-made object in orbit.

More than 100 people visited Mir during its 15 years in space. For some of them, it was their home for several months. The visitors carried out lots of experiments and increased our understanding of what happens to the human body after a long time spent in space.

During Mir's lifetime, the political world back on Earth changed dramatically. In 1991, the Soviet Union fell apart when its leader, Mikhail Gorbachev, stepped down, and Russia and several other nations were formed. The cosmonauts on board Mir at that time returned home to a very different country. This change led to a new collaboration in space between the United States and Russia. Both the US Space Shuttle and the Russian Soyuz took people to Mir, and the two countries began working together in space regularly.

Key

1 **Progress spacecraft**
The spacecraft was used to carry supplies, but not crew, to Mir.

2 **Solar arrays**
These panels used sunlight to generate power.

3 **Core module**
This was the heart of the space station. It contained the living quarters.

4 **Kristall docking module**
This allowed the NASA Space Shuttle to dock with Mir.

5 **Kvant-2**
This module had an airlock used for spacewalks.

6 **Soyuz spacecraft**
This Russian spacecraft was used to take crew and supplies to Mir.

Life on Mir
Cosmonauts and astronauts a group photo. Life on Mir h including a dangerous fire ir

Dining in space
NASA astronauts enjoy some Russian food while on board Mir. They are eating food out of tins because it's hard to cook meals in space.

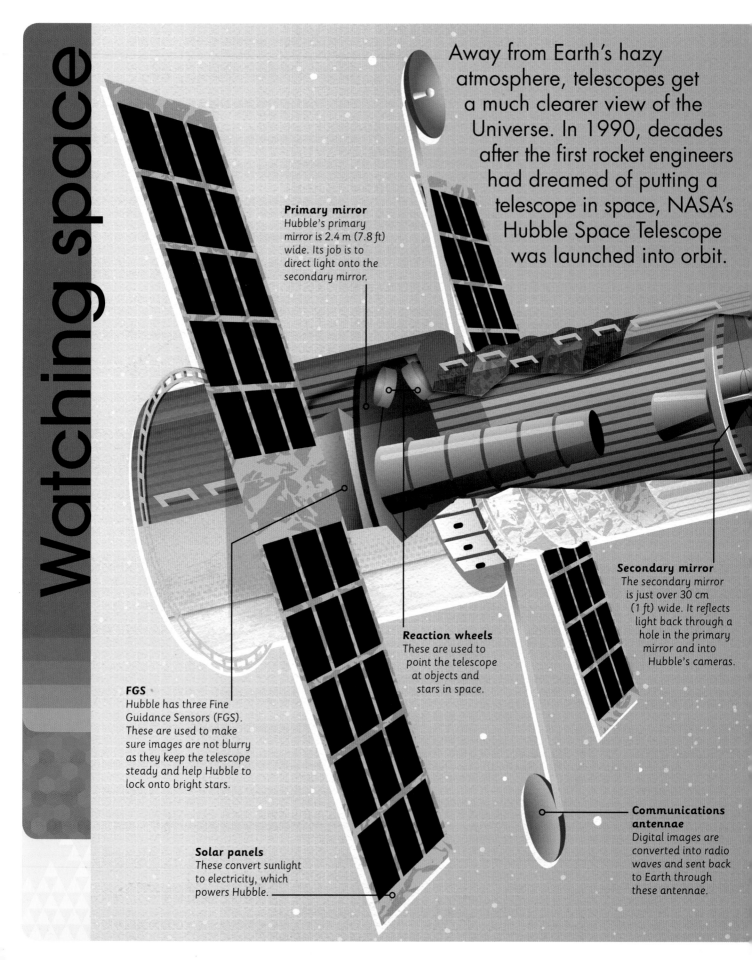

Away from Earth's hazy atmosphere, telescopes get a much clearer view of the Universe. In 1990, decades after the first rocket engineers had dreamed of putting a telescope in space, NASA's Hubble Space Telescope was launched into orbit.

Primary mirror
Hubble's primary mirror is 2.4 m (7.8 ft) wide. Its job is to direct light onto the secondary mirror.

Secondary mirror
The secondary mirror is just over 30 cm (1 ft) wide. It reflects light back through a hole in the primary mirror and into Hubble's cameras.

Reaction wheels
These are used to point the telescope at objects and stars in space.

FGS
Hubble has three Fine Guidance Sensors (FGS). These are used to make sure images are not blurry as they keep the telescope steady and help Hubble to lock onto bright stars.

Solar panels
These convert sunlight to electricity, which powers Hubble.

Communications antennae
Digital images are converted into radio waves and sent back to Earth through these antennae.

Aperture door
If needed, the
aperture door
can close to prevent
bright sunlight
from damaging
the telescope.

Servicing Hubble

To service the Hubble Telescope,
the Space Shuttle flew
alongside it, took hold of it
with a robotic arm, and put it
in the Shuttle's cargo bay. From
here, astronauts could repair it
and replace faulty parts.

Photos

The Hubble Space Telescope has given us
some of the most incredible pictures of the
Universe. It has taken hundreds of thousands
of photos, which show stars being born
and galaxies that are really far away.

Tarantula Nebula
This photo is of one
of the Milky Way's
nearest neighbours,
the Tarantula Nebula.

Lagoon Nebula
Taken to celebrate Hubble's
28th birthday, this photo
centres on a star that is
200,000 times brighter
than our Sun.

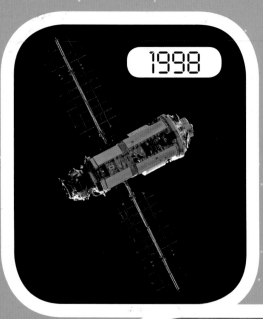

1998

Zarya
The first part of the space station, or module, to be launched was Zarya. Built in Russia, it provided electrical power and storage during the assembly of the ISS.

2005

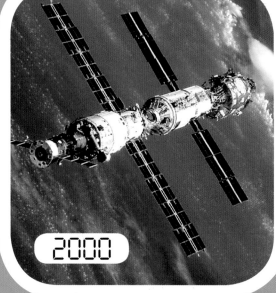

Adding Zvezda
Zvezda was the third module to be added to the ISS. It contains life support systems and living-quarters for two crew members.

2000

Getting bigger
By 2005, the ISS had a science laboratory, airlocks, and Canadarm2 – a robotic arm for moving equipment around.

Further expansion
More solar panels were added to the ISS in 2007. These collect sunlight, which is converted into electricity.

In 1998, construction of the International Space Station (ISS) began. It was built piece by piece in orbit, and different parts were launched into space by both Russia and the United States. Astronauts and cosmonauts completed difficult spacewalks where they installed modules, rewired systems, and made repairs to the outside of the ISS.

Space began to change from being a source of competition to a place where different countries could work together – even if they didn't get on with each other on Earth!

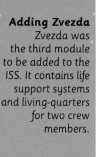

Building a space station

2010

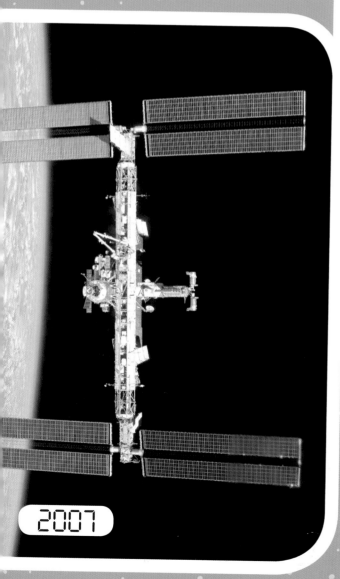

2007

A new module
*The space station is bigger than a football pitch!
It is the biggest human-made object to orbit Earth.*

In total, 15 countries worked on the project. The result was the world's largest outpost in space, orbiting at a height of around 400 km (250 miles) above the Earth. Since 2 November 2000, it has been continually occupied by people working in space.

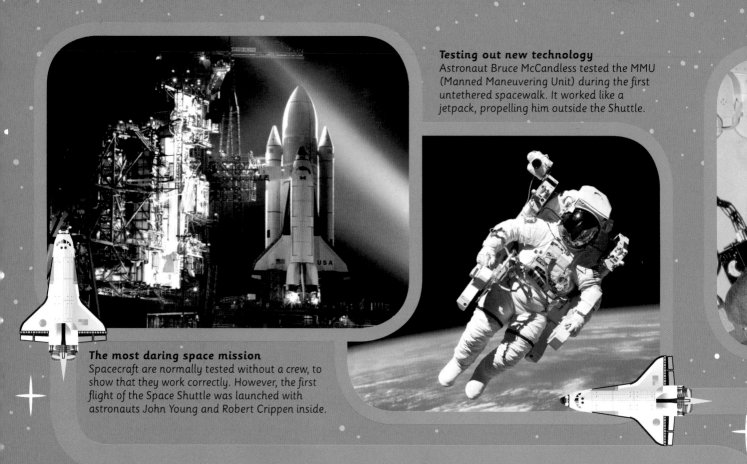

Testing out new technology
Astronaut Bruce McCandless tested the MMU (Manned Maneuvering Unit) during the first untethered spacewalk. It worked like a jetpack, propelling him outside the Shuttle.

The most daring space mission
Spacecraft are normally tested without a crew, to show that they work correctly. However, the first flight of the Space Shuttle was launched with astronauts John Young and Robert Crippen inside.

Space workhorse

NASA produced a fleet of five reusable spacecraft: Columbia, Challenger, Discovery, Atlantis, and Endeavour. These were the Space Shuttles, and they took part in 135 missions over 30 years. The Shuttle programme helped to build the ISS, launch and service the Hubble Space Telescope, and took 355 astronauts from across the globe into orbit.

One of the most complex pieces of machinery ever built, the Space Shuttle did lots of work during its 30 years of service. It was used to carry out science experiments and launch satellites. It was also able to send other robotic spacecraft deeper into our Solar System to understand more about other planets. The Shuttle sent Magellan to Venus and Galileo to orbit Jupiter.

The lessons learned from those 135 missions have helped to lay the foundations for future space explorers.

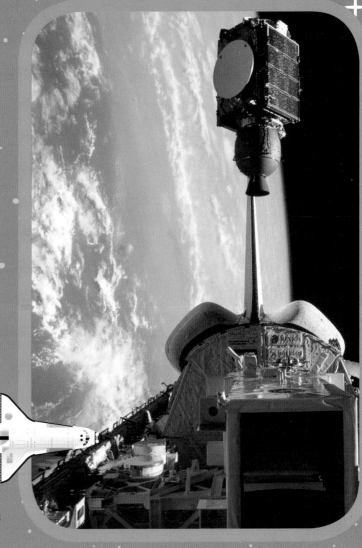

Medical advances
Astronaut Norman Thagard may have looked like an alien, but he was actually studying how the human body reacts to space travel.

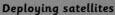

Deploying satellites
The payload bay of the shuttle carried many satellites to space. Astronauts could then make sure the satellites were placed in Earth's orbit correctly.

Space Shuttle tragedies

Unfortunately, travelling in a Space Shuttle was very dangerous. Two crews, with a total of 14 astronauts, lost their lives in separate disasters — Challenger in 1986 and Columbia in 2003.

Challenger crew

Columbia crew

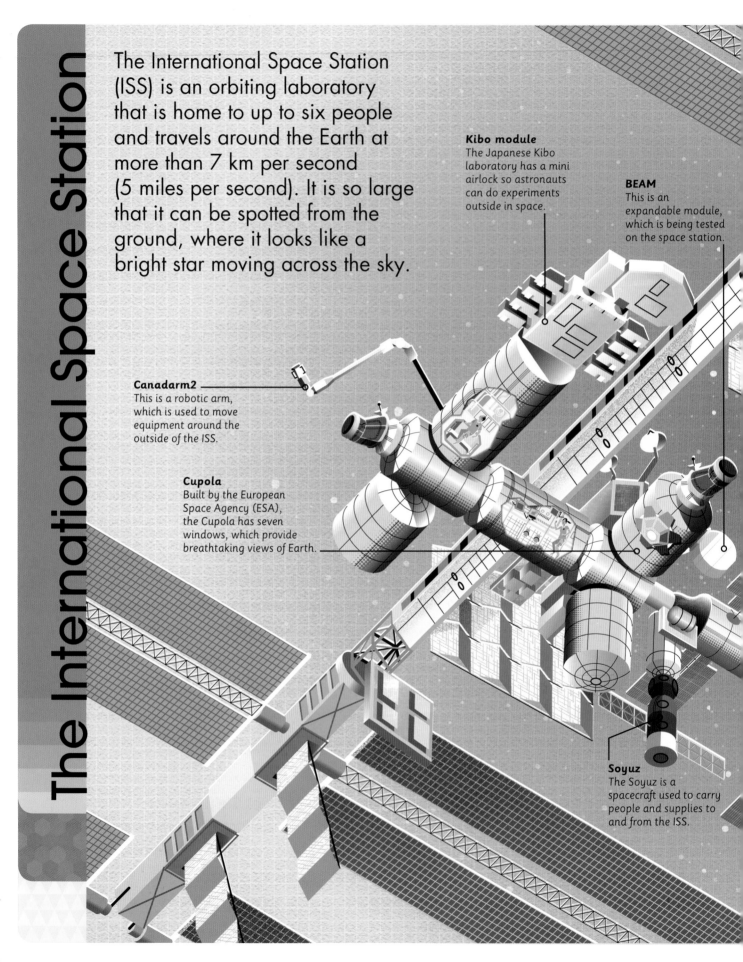

The International Space Station (ISS) is an orbiting laboratory that is home to up to six people and travels around the Earth at more than 7 km per second (5 miles per second). It is so large that it can be spotted from the ground, where it looks like a bright star moving across the sky.

Kibo module
The Japanese Kibo laboratory has a mini airlock so astronauts can do experiments outside in space.

BEAM
This is an expandable module, which is being tested on the space station.

Canadarm2
This is a robotic arm, which is used to move equipment around the outside of the ISS.

Cupola
Built by the European Space Agency (ESA), the Cupola has seven windows, which provide breathtaking views of Earth.

Soyuz
The Soyuz is a spacecraft used to carry people and supplies to and from the ISS.

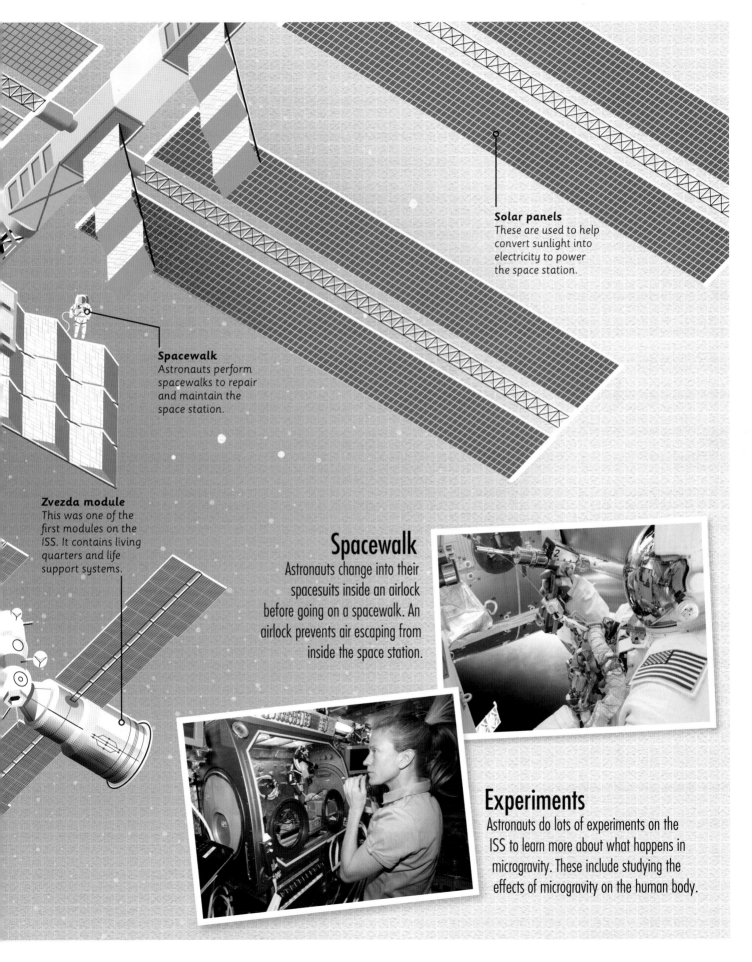

Solar panels
These are used to help convert sunlight into electricity to power the space station.

Spacewalk
Astronauts perform spacewalks to repair and maintain the space station.

Zvezda module
This was one of the first modules on the ISS. It contains living quarters and life support systems.

Spacewalk
Astronauts change into their spacesuits inside an airlock before going on a spacewalk. An airlock prevents air escaping from inside the space station.

Experiments
Astronauts do lots of experiments on the ISS to learn more about what happens in microgravity. These include studying the effects of microgravity on the human body.

Living in space

For astronauts on board the ISS, space is their home. Most missions last several months and some astronauts stay for a year! Scientists have found ways of doing everyday tasks in the microgravity of space.

Staying clean
With no shower on the ISS, washing your hair is complicated. It involves using a pouch of water, shampoo you don't have to rinse out, a towel, and lots of patience as the water can float away.

Catherine Coleman

Samantha Cristoforetti

Exercising
Astronauts have to do daily exercise in space to keep their muscles and bones in good shape. This is the treadmill used by astronauts on the space station — it comes with a harness that stops them floating away when they're running.

Music
To wake up astronauts on the ISS, NASA uses music. There is even a guitar on the space station, which Chris Hadfield (left) used when he recorded an album in space.

Chris Hadfield

Going to the toilet
This photograph shows what the toilet looks like on the ISS. Astronauts have to fasten themselves to the seat so they don't float away, and a vacuum device sucks away waste.

Food
In space, most of the food eaten has to have water added to it first. There is some fresh food available however, such as fruit, which is brought to the ISS by resupply ships or new astronauts.

Tim Peake

Peggy Whitson

Admiring the view
Astronauts get some free time on the ISS. They can watch films, read books, and send emails back home, but one of the most popular things to do is to look out of the window at Earth.

119

The Soyuz rocket

TOYS
A Russian tradition is to bring a cuddly toy on each space mission. The toy is a mascot for the mission, but it also indicates when the crew have reached weightlessness as it begins to float around!

When the Space Shuttle program stopped in July 2011, the Russian Soyuz rocket became the only way for people to get to the International Space Station (ISS).

First introduced in 1966, the Soyuz has been launched more times than any other type of rocket. Different versions of the Soyuz rocket are also used on uncrewed flights to send supplies to the ISS and to launch satellites.

When a crewed Soyuz rocket launches, three people sit at the top of the rocket inside the Soyuz spacecraft. It's really small, so they have to squeeze

Squeezed into Soyuz
The only part of the Soyuz that returns to Earth is the Descent Module. There isn't much room inside!

Landing
After re-entry to Earth, a parachute is used to slow down the Soyuz's Descent Module, and engines fire to soften the landing.

in tight. The Soyuz took its first crew to the ISS in November 2000. Since then, there has always been a Soyuz spacecraft stationed at the ISS, acting as a lifeboat back to Earth in case of an emergency.

Space travellers that launch on the Soyuz follow the traditions started by Yuri Gagarin. These include doing a wee by the back tyre of the bus that takes them to the launch pad, and planting a tree before the mission.

Rocket launch

Within a matter of hours the Soyuz spacecraft docks with the ISS.

The Soyuz spacecraft unfolds its solar panels and begins its journey to dock with the ISS.

At around 200 km (124 miles), the third stage cuts off. The crew now experience weightlessness.

At 180 km (111 miles), the second stage separates and the third stage ignites to give the crew the last push they need to get to orbit.

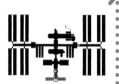

After two minutes the first stage, the boosters, burn up and are ejected. The spacecraft's cover is dumped 30 seconds later.

The Soyuz rocket and crew launch from Baikonur, Kazakhstan.

The Soyuz rocket is very reliable. It has three parts, or stages, which are used to get the Soyuz spacecraft into orbit. It takes just nine minutes from lift-off for the crew to reach space!

Flying a spaceship

One of the most exciting things astronauts can do is fly a spaceship. At NASA, if you want to become a commander you must first become a pilot astronaut.

It is difficult to learn how to fly in space because of something called orbital mechanics. When you are in space, you have to slow down to go faster and speed up to slow down, which can be confusing!

Piloting the Space Shuttle involved three methods of flying. At launch astronauts flew a rocket, in space they flew a satellite, and when returning to Earth they flew an aeroplane.

Chris Ferguson

Commander for the final Space Shuttle mission

"To command the final Space Shuttle mission was an honour. I consider it one of those special moments in life. Now with Boeing, flying the Starliner as part of NASA's commercial crew, I am using my experience for the next generation of space missions."

Space Shuttle control panel

1 Windows
These were made of three layers of glass to protect the astronauts.

2 Orbital readings
The astronauts monitor the condition of their orbital engines and computers here.

3 Plug panel
Laptops are positioned here to assist in activities such as reading the flight plan.

4 Switches
Switches were used to help control the vehicle.

5 Monitors
These gave astronauts information about the spacecraft.

Eileen Collins

First female Space Shuttle Pilot and first female Space Shuttle Commander

"Initially it is difficult to learn how to fly, but once you learn how the Space Shuttle flies and complete the training, it actually becomes quite fun and easy. As a pilot, I enjoyed flying the Space Shuttle because it was very responsive. As a Commander, I enjoyed the responsibility of leading a crew."

Being an astronaut doesn't always mean being in space. In fact, for most of the time, they work here on Earth. Astronauts have to train for a long time before going into space. They also help out on other missions, such as working in mission control as CAPCOM (capsule communicator).

One of the most exciting jobs astronauts do on Earth is live underwater. Nicknamed "aquanauts", they work with professional divers, scientists, and engineers under the ocean. This project is called NASA Extreme Environment Mission Operations, or NEEMO for short. Aquanauts spend up to four weeks living inside the underwater base Aquarius, which is located 19 m (62 ft) below the ocean surface, off the coast of Florida, USA. NEEMO is

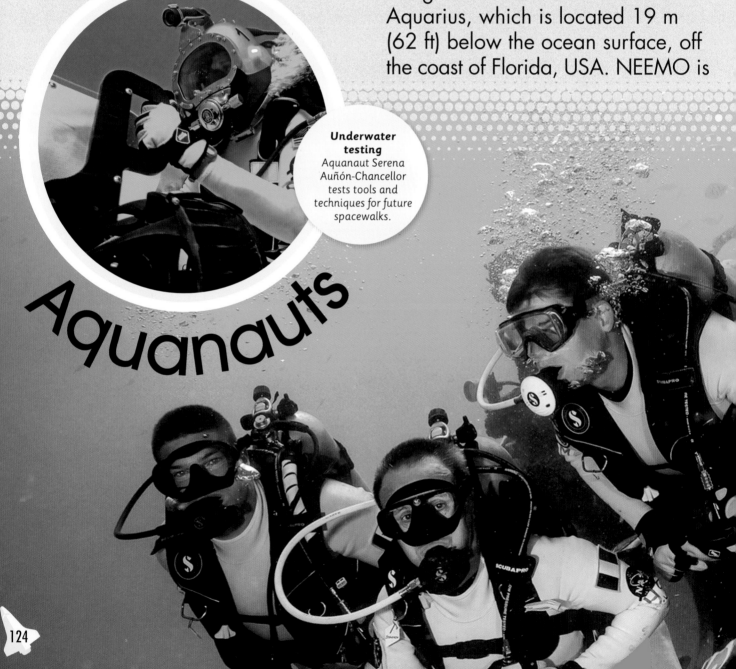

Underwater testing
Aquanaut Serena Auñón-Chancellor tests tools and techniques for future spacewalks.

Aquanauts

hugely important. It helps NASA and other space agencies prepare to explore different places in space.

Inside Aquarius, there are bunk beds for the aquanauts to sleep in, a table to eat at, and places to carry out experiments and research. Although still on Earth, this base is a completely alien environment for humans to be in. Here, aquanauts face some of the same challenges that people would encounter living on the Moon, an asteroid, or another planet.

Aquanauts train for future space missions by going outside the base to collect "soil" samples and test "spacewalking" techniques. The underwater conditions are similar to weightlessness in space.

Downtime
Aquanauts Tim Peake and Steve Squyres take a break and use their tablets, watched by some curious fish!

Inside and outside
Two aquanauts look out while six others pose outside Aquarius during a NEEMO mission.

Visiting other worlds

Robotic spacecraft have been incredibly important in learning more about our Solar System. While it might seem like we know a lot about space, we actually know very little – and the more we discover, the more questions we have.

As humans have focused on missions in Earth's orbit, these spacecraft, built by lots of different countries, have travelled billions of kilometres to explore deeper into space. They've revisited our Moon and journeyed to comets and the gas giants. Along the way they've discovered possible liquid oceans on other moons and listened to the eerie sounds of Jupiter's powerful atmosphere.

They are our eyes and ears into the Universe. Travelling to places humans cannot yet visit, they are continually rewriting our understanding of space.

Jade Rabbit on the Moon
China's Yuto ("Jade Rabbit") rover landed on the Moon in 2013. Yuto was controlled from Earth and sent back incredible colour photos.

Mickey Mouse on Mercury
Mickey Mouse was spotted on the planet Mercury – or rather, a group of craters that look like him! They were discovered by NASA's Messenger spacecraft.

Craters on Venus

This crater was caused by a meteorite hitting the surface of Venus. Data from two Soviet Venera missions and NASA's Magellan mission were used to create this image.

Titan's surface

Saturn's moon Titan has an atmosphere and is a little like a young Earth. When the European Huygens spacecraft landed here, it discovered a world with an orange sky and a sticky, clay-like surface.

Philae lander

The Philae lander travelled across our Solar System with the European Space Agency's (ESA) Rosetta spacecraft, before landing on the surface of a comet in 2014!

LEGO® Minifigures aboard Juno

LEGO® Minifigures have been to Jupiter! Minifigures of the god Jupiter, his wife Juno, and scientist Galileo Galilei travelled to the giant planet in NASA's Juno spacecraft.

Jupiter's south pole

Jupiter's south pole is beautiful, but you wouldn't want to live there. The oval shapes are powerful cyclones up to 1,000 km (620 miles) wide. They were discovered by NASA's Juno spacecraft.

Saturn's rings

Imagine diving through Saturn's rings. That's exactly what NASA's Cassini spacecraft did! The rings are made mostly of lumps of ice, ranging in size from a grain of sand to a mountain.

Cameras
Curiosity has 17 cameras, 7 of which are located on its "head". They act as the rover's "eyes".

Scientific equipment
Equipment on the rover's body includes a chemistry lab and an antenna to communicate with people back on Earth.

Curiosity's selfie
In this photograph, the arm holding the camera has been edited out. When the rover takes a self-portrait, multiple images are taken, which are then stitched together to create the portrait.

Wheels
Big grippy wheels help Curiosity keep stable as it explores the surface of Mars.

Robots on Mars

One of the most exciting places robotic spacecraft have visited is Mars. They first started exploring the Red Planet in the 1970s, when NASA sent its two Viking probes. They performed "soft landings" – landings that don't damage the spacecraft – on the Martian surface and took colour photographs to show us what Mars looks like.

Today Mars is a planet occupied by robots. Controlled from Earth, they drive around taking photographs and doing experiments. With the help of spacecraft orbiting around the planet, they are looking for water, past signs of life, and perhaps even evidence of simple life forms that might still exist today. One of the most famous robot residents is NASA's Curiosity rover, which has roamed the planet since 2012, studying Martian soil and rock samples.

Robots will continue to explore Mars – until we're ready to send people there instead...

Mars Atmosphere and Volatile EvolutioN (MAVEN)

NASA's MAVEN spacecraft orbits around Mars. Launched in 2013, its aim is to find out more about the history of Mars's atmosphere and climate. It is also trying to discover whether the planet can support life. This image shows an artist's impression of the spacecraft in orbit.

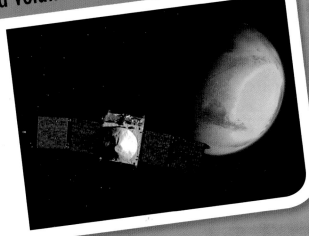

Early image of Pluto
The best image of Pluto we had before the New Horizons mission was this fuzzy photograph taken by the Hubble Space Telescope.

Kuiper belt
The Kuiper belt is a doughnut-shaped region at the edge of our Solar System. This cold, dark place is home to trillions of icy objects and comets, and some dwarf planets.

New Horizons spacecraft
An artist's drawing of the New Horizons spacecraft as it approaches Pluto. The dish is used to communicate with Earth.

New Horizons

The New Horizons mission to Pluto and the Kuiper belt is showing us worlds beyond our imagination. It's the story of an incredible journey to the edge of our Solar System.

When the New Horizons spacecraft was launched in 2006, Pluto was still known as a planet. A few months later, it was reclassified as a dwarf planet. New Horizons reached Pluto – its first destination – in 2015, after travelling 4.8 billion km (3 billion miles) from Earth. Pluto had once been dismissed as a "boring lump of rock", but the spacecraft discovered an amazing world. It had a gigantic heart-shaped region of frozen nitrogen, now named Tombaugh Regio. There were

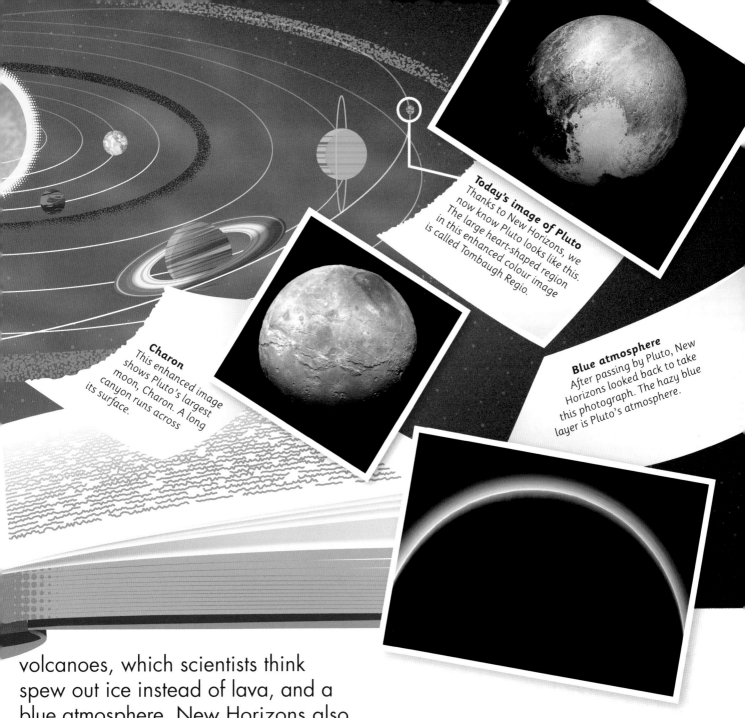

Today's image of Pluto
Thanks to New Horizons, we now know Pluto looks like this. The large heart-shaped region in this enhanced colour image is called Tombaugh Regio.

Charon
This enhanced image shows Pluto's largest moon, Charon. A long canyon runs across its surface.

Blue atmosphere
After passing by Pluto, New Horizons looked back to take this photograph. The hazy blue layer is Pluto's atmosphere.

volcanoes, which scientists think spew out ice instead of lava, and a blue atmosphere. New Horizons also sent back images of Pluto's moons.

The New Horizons spacecraft is still exploring the Kuiper belt. It's travelling to the furthest reaches of our Solar System, and the story of what we will find is only just beginning…

"People will know about this mission for centuries to come." – Alan Stern, Principal Investigator of the New Horizons mission

Planet hunting

We are living in an age of discovery about space. Recently, we've learned that when you look up at the night sky, almost every star you can see has one or more planets orbiting around it. Planets that orbit around other stars are called exoplanets. For a long time, people wondered whether such planets existed, but it took until the 1990s for the first confirmed detection.

We now also know that many stars other than our Sun have multiple planets – the Universe is teeming with solar systems. We have even found planets that don't orbit around a star. Known as rogue planets, they wander the Universe alone.

Some exoplanets are gas giants, even more gigantic than Jupiter. There are water worlds and even a planet made mostly of diamond! Just imagine what else could be out there.

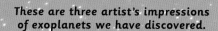

These are three artist's impressions
of exoplanets we have discovered.

Kepler-20e
This planet is similar
in size to Earth.
However, it is too
close to its star for
liquid water to exist
on its surface.

Kepler space telescope

One of the ways we have found exoplanets
is by using a space telescope called Kepler.
This telescope can detect planets because
the light of the parent star dips very slightly
when an orbiting planet passes in front of it.

HD 219134 b
About 1.6 times
bigger than Earth,
this planet may be
rocky and volcanic.
It orbits its star in
just three days!

Space was once a tale of two powerful nations: the Soviet Union and the United States. Today, it is a tale of nearly every person on Earth.

Space exploration is now global, and the number of countries involved is growing every year. Going to space is no longer just about government-owned space agencies such as NASA – commercial companies, who plan to make money from space travel, and individuals are now involved.

Our journey into space is not too different from how pioneers like Christopher Columbus explored the Earth. He sailed to the Americas in 1492 and inspired more Europeans to cross the oceans. Similarly, space race pioneers, such as Yuri Gagarin and Neil Armstrong, inspired us to travel to space.

These space heroes laid the foundations for countries, companies, and individuals to head into orbit.

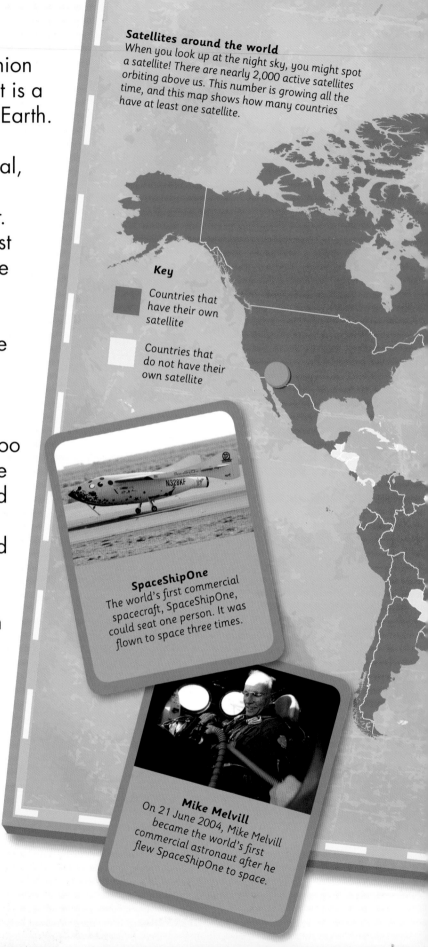

Satellites around the world
When you look up at the night sky, you might spot a satellite! There are nearly 2,000 active satellites orbiting above us. This number is growing all the time, and this map shows how many countries have at least one satellite.

Key
Countries that have their own satellite

Countries that do not have their own satellite

SpaceShipOne
The world's first commercial spacecraft, SpaceShipOne, could seat one person. It was flown to space three times.

Mike Melvill
On 21 June 2004, Mike Melvill became the world's first commercial astronaut after he flew SpaceShipOne to space.

The new space race

NASA's commercial crew
Astronauts from NASA can now fly to space from the United States in privately-built commercial space capsules, which take them to Earth's orbit and the ISS.

India's Mars Orbiter Mission
In 2013, India launched its first mission to Mars. The Mars Orbiter spacecraft studies the planet's atmosphere and surface.

Galileo satellite system
Galileo is a global navigation system made up of 26 satellites. It was created by the European Space Agency (ESA).

Nigerian satellites
Nigeria has a growing network of satellites. They are used for communications and to help provide internet access to rural areas.

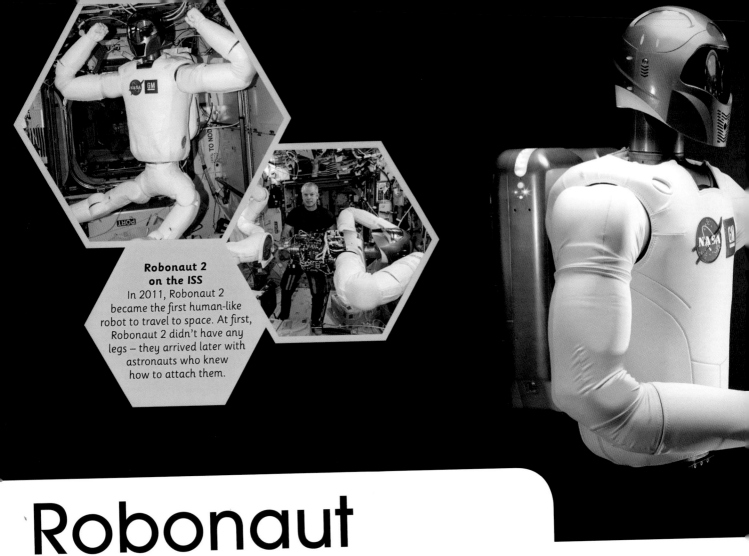

Robonaut 2 on the ISS
In 2011, Robonaut 2 became the first human-like robot to travel to space. At first, Robonaut 2 didn't have any legs – they arrived later with astronauts who knew how to attach them.

Robonaut

Ever wondered what it would feel like to shake hands with a robot? Well, astronauts already know.

Meet Robonaut. Robonaut is a robotic helper designed and built by NASA. A version of Robonaut, called Robonaut 2, even lived in space, on board the International Space Station. Robonaut is a humanoid robot, as it was designed with similar features to humans. Robonauts can help astronauts by doing time-consuming chores, repetitive tasks (they don't get bored), and helping with dangerous jobs.

As we continue to explore deeper into space, robotic crew members are going to become very important. Versions of Robonaut could be sent to new places before humans – to

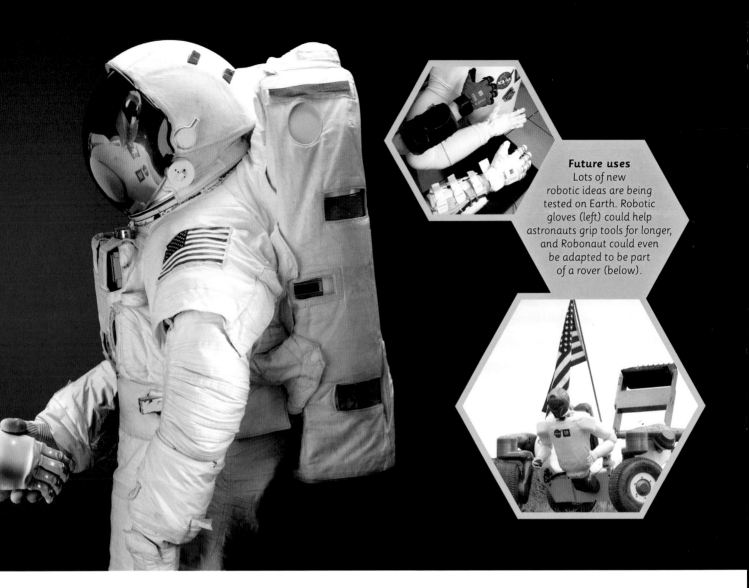

Future uses
Lots of new robotic ideas are being tested on Earth. Robotic gloves (left) could help astronauts grip tools for longer, and Robonaut could even be adapted to be part of a rover (below).

set up tools, living quarters, and experiments so that everything is ready for when humans arrive. Robonauts could also be adapted to have wheels instead of feet so that they can move around quickly.

Future astronauts could even wear robotic clothing, which would give them robot-like abilities. NASA has already developed robotic gloves, which could help spacewalking astronauts, and in the future, astronauts could wear entire robotic suits – known as exoskeletons. These suits could give the wearer improved mobility and strength, and they could also help people who are unable to walk to move again. In fact, all of the robotics being developed for space could improve life for people on Earth.

Super mega-rockets

Introducing the new class of rockets. These aren't just mega-rockets, these are super mega-rockets, part of a new generation with the potential to help humans have even greater adventures in space.

New Glenn 3-stage

Blue Origin's New Glenn 3-stage rocket is 99 m (326 ft) tall. It will be used by Blue Origin to help more people access space.

Delta IV Heavy

Manufactured by United Launch Alliance, the Delta IV Heavy rocket's achievements include launching the Parker Solar Probe to "touch" the Sun in 2018. At 72 m (236 ft) tall, this super mega-rocket is reliable and powerful.

Falcon Heavy

Standing at a height of 70 m (230 ft) is SpaceX's Falcon Heavy rocket. It launched a car into space in 2018, and its boosters, which give the rocket extra power at launch, can land back on Earth to be reused.

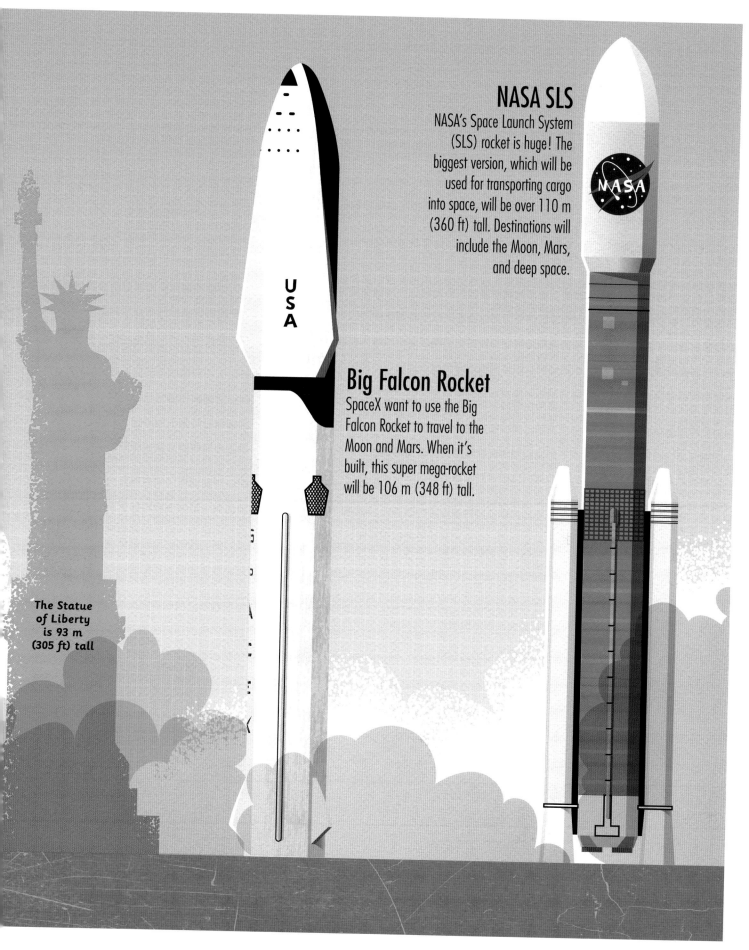

NASA SLS

NASA's Space Launch System (SLS) rocket is huge! The biggest version, which will be used for transporting cargo into space, will be over 110 m (360 ft) tall. Destinations will include the Moon, Mars, and deep space.

Big Falcon Rocket

SpaceX want to use the Big Falcon Rocket to travel to the Moon and Mars. When it's built, this super mega-rocket will be 106 m (348 ft) tall.

USA

The Statue of Liberty is 93 m (305 ft) tall

Landing back on Earth

When you travel by aeroplane, it isn't thrown away after just one flight. However, for a long time, that's exactly what happened with space rockets. Now, new rockets are being developed that can launch satellites and spacecraft to orbit and then land back on Earth on either a landing pad or a barge in the ocean. For some missions, landing on a barge at sea is necessary as the rockets don't have enough fuel left to make it back to a landing pad.

One of the biggest obstacles facing future space exploration is cost. It is very expensive

Reusable rocket

While it might look like this is a rocket taking off, it's actually the first stage of SpaceX's Falcon 9 rocket landing back on Earth.

to launch rockets that send people and experiments to space.

While the Space Shuttle fleet was reusable, it cost a lot to operate – an average of $450 million per mission.

Companies like SpaceX and Blue Origin are creating new reusable rockets that will make it easier and cheaper to access space. This is great news for people who want to go to space, or have ideas for new experiments that could be done in orbit.

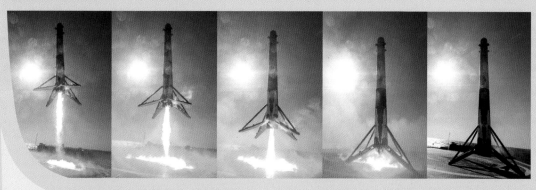

Perfect landing

One of the companies perfecting landing rockets back on Earth is SpaceX. The first stage of their Falcon 9 rocket has to slow from speeds of 2.4 km per second (1.5 miles per second) to ensure a safe landing.

How it works

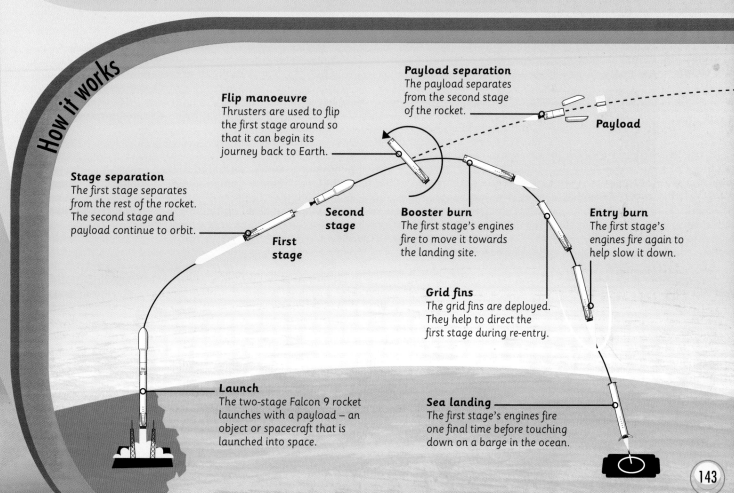

Payload separation
The payload separates from the second stage of the rocket.

Payload

Flip manoeuvre
Thrusters are used to flip the first stage around so that it can begin its journey back to Earth.

Stage separation
The first stage separates from the rest of the rocket. The second stage and payload continue to orbit.

Second stage

First stage

Booster burn
The first stage's engines fire to move it towards the landing site.

Entry burn
The first stage's engines fire again to help slow it down.

Grid fins
The grid fins are deployed. They help to direct the first stage during re-entry.

Launch
The two-stage Falcon 9 rocket launches with a payload – an object or spacecraft that is launched into space.

Sea landing
The first stage's engines fire one final time before touching down on a barge in the ocean.

Musk vs

Elon Musk and Jeff Bezos are two of the richest people on the planet. They are both passionate about space travel and are using their wealth to change the way we explore space.

Elon Musk has a company called SpaceX. He founded it because he thinks that a future in which people are exploring the stars is much more exciting than one in which they are not. SpaceX works with NASA to send supplies, and also astronauts, in its Dragon space capsules to the International Space Station (ISS).

However, Elon's ultimate goal is Mars. He wants to send humans there and eventually colonize the Red Planet.

SpaceX car

In 2018, Elon Musk launched his car into space! Strapped into the driver's seat was a dummy in a spacesuit, nicknamed "Starman". The car was a test load for the first flight of SpaceX's Falcon Heavy rocket.

Bezos

Jeff Bezos's motto is *gradatim ferociter*, which is Latin for "step by step, ferociously". He uses this approach for his space company, called Blue Origin, step by step working to improve technology. The aim is to make it cheaper to go to space – for astronauts and tourists too.

Jeff also wants to move factories off the Earth. They'd be powered by the Sun and wouldn't pollute our planet. His vision is to have millions of people living and working in space.

Elon and Jeff share something in common – they had ideas that at the time seemed impossible, but they turned them into reality. Together they are shaping a new space age.

Blue Origin New Shepard spacecraft

Named after the astronaut Alan Shepard – the first American to go to space – New Shepard is a reusable launch vehicle. The rocket takes off and lands vertically, and it has been designed to take tourists on space trips.

Space junk

Everywhere humans go, we seem to leave rubbish in our wake, and space is no different. There are more than 500,000 pieces of junk, which are larger than a marble, orbiting around our planet. There are bits of used rockets, broken satellite parts, and even tools that astronauts may have lost during spacewalks.

One of the biggest problems is that as the number of objects orbiting Earth increases, so do the chances of a collision. When two pieces of junk collide, even more junk is created when the pieces break up and become smaller.

Even small pieces of junk can cause problems. Hurtling around Earth at speeds of up to 28,000 kph (17,500 mph), small pieces of space junk have the potential to cause serious damage to the ISS or the many satellites people on Earth rely on.

As we continue to go to space, one of the biggest questions we need to answer is "How do we clean up all of this mess?" If we don't, we could put future missions in danger.

Falling back to Earth

Space junk can re-enter the Earth's atmosphere, and while most pieces will burn up, occasionally they survive re-entry. This is a rocket's fuel tank that landed in Texas, USA.

How to clean up space

At the end of their mission, modern satellites are designed to burn up in Earth's atmosphere or move out of the way of active satellites. However, older satellites remain in space. One idea for cleaning up these satellites is to use a net to capture them. Another method is to grab the old satellites with harpoons and reel them in. They would be removed from orbit by being sent to burn up in Earth's atmosphere.

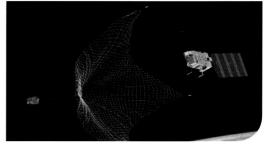

Catching a satellite in a net

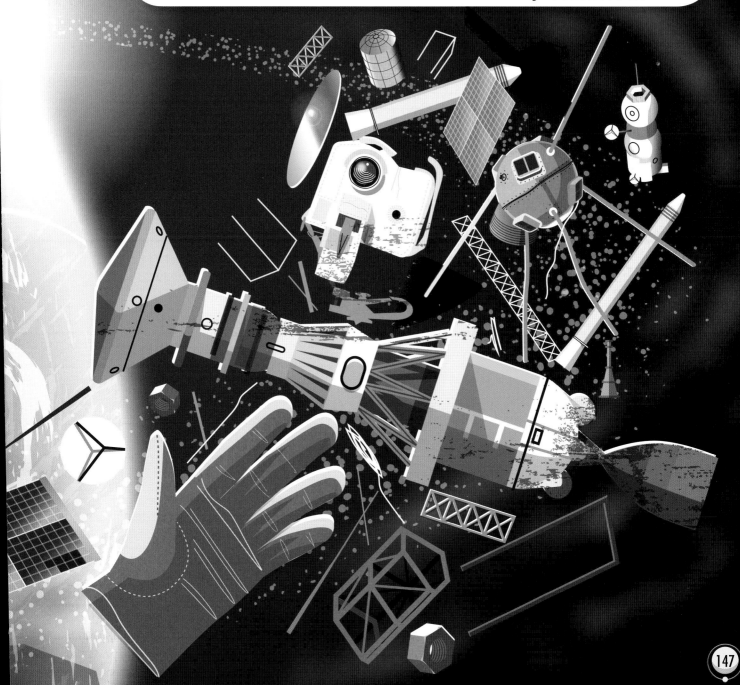

A new space nation

There are now three nations that can launch people into space: the United States, Russia, and China. Ancient Chinese legends used to talk about people travelling to space, and China has a long history with rocketry and astronomy. At the start of the 21st century, China finally sent a person into space.

In China, an astronaut is known as a taikonaut [tie-ko-naut].

China's Long March 2F rocket prepares for launch in 2011

Yang Liwei
In 2003, Yang Liwei became the first person to be sent to space by the Chinese space programme. He launched into space on board the Shenzhou 5 spacecraft.

Liu Yang
The first Chinese woman to travel to space was Liu Yang. She orbited the Earth in 2012 as part of the crew of Shenzhou 9.

Taikonauts travel to space in a spacecraft called the Shenzhou, which means "divine vessel". Just like in the United States and Russia, the Chinese have different types of rocket for different missions.

As well as sending people and satellites into space, the China National Space Administration (CNSA) set its sights on the Moon. It sent an unmanned spacecraft called Chang'e 1 to orbit the Moon in 2007, and was able to explore the surface of the Moon in 2013, using a robotic spacecraft called Yutu.

In the future, China plans to send more spacecraft to explore the Moon, including the far side. It also wants to send spacecraft to explore Mars and the outer gas planets in our Solar System.

Tiangong-1 space station

Tiangong-1 was China's first space station, which orbited the Earth from 2011 to 2018. The size of a school bus, it was used to host two different crews of taikonauts.

Back to the Moon

Lunar soil could be used to cover the Moon base, protecting the people inside from the Sun's radiation.

This artist's impression shows the "Moon village" that is being planned by the European Space Agency (ESA) as a successor to the ISS.

One day, when you look up at the Moon, there will be people living and working there. When NASA's Apollo missions ended in 1972, nobody believed that we wouldn't go back for so long. Instead, we made huge steps learning how to live in space – in space stations orbiting around the Earth. The knowledge gained from this will help us put people – men, and for the first time, women – back on the Moon. However, this time it won't just be for short visits. We'll build a permanent base there. The Moon is only three days away from Earth, so it can be used to test out the technology we need to send people to other planets.

Space agencies and private companies are already exploring how to make this happen.

Astronauts will be able to look up at the Earth — just like you look up at the Moon!

New Lunar Rover

When we return to the Moon, we'll need a car like the Lunar Rover used for the Apollo missions. NASA is exploring ideas for vehicles that could be used by future astronauts and explorers.

Astronauts will wear spacesuits similar to the Apollo spacesuits, but with more advanced technology.

Robots will help people on the Moon. This robot-operated 3D printer could help create the lunar base.

★ Apollo 11

★ Apollo 12

★ Apollo 14

★ Apollo 15

MOON MUSEUM
ADMITS ONE

★ Apollo 16

★ Apollo 17

★ Lunar Rover

★

Moon Museum

The Apollo landing sites, with all the objects and signs of activity left by the astronauts, still remain on the Moon. With no weather on the Moon, the astronauts' footsteps will last for thousands of years. Future Moon explorers will be able to visit these sites. They could become an "off-world" museum, honouring the ground-breaking achievements of the Apollo missions.

How to move to space

The distance from the ground on Earth to space is around 100 km (62 miles). Space isn't that far away, but there are lots of challenges to overcome if you want to move there.

On Earth, we have everything we need to survive, such as air to breathe and food to eat. If you are sick you can visit a doctor, if you're thirsty you can turn on a tap to get water, and Earth's atmosphere protects us from harmful radiation from space.

On the International Space Station (ISS), astronauts are supported by supplies sent from Earth – including air, water, fuel, and food. In an emergency, they can travel back to Earth quite quickly. However, in order to explore deeper into space, future explorers will need to be able to support themselves.

1 Food and water
We won't be able to take much food with us when we explore space, so we need to learn how to grow plants in microgravity. As for water – astronauts already recycle their urine to drink on the ISS!

3 Staying healthy
Astronauts will need to take medical supplies with them in case of emergencies far away from Earth. Some people will also need to be trained to perform operations in space should an accident happen.

An artist's impression of how NASA plans to extract water from the soil on Mars.

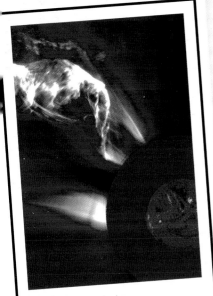

5 Isolation training

On a long space mission, it will just be you and your crew completely alone. In order to understand how isolation affects humans, astronauts practise on Earth in extreme environments, such as in Antarctica.

2 Protection from radiation

Charged particles from the Sun pose a radiation threat to space travellers. One of the best ways to protect astronauts is to put a layer of water around the spacecraft. Plastic can also be used for added protection.

4 Learning to live off the land

On Earth we have learned to use the resources available to us, like water and soil. We will need to do this on the Moon and Mars to survive.

6 Homes in space

Future astronauts could live in pop-up homes, which can be expanded in space. These homes take up a small amount of room on a space rocket, meaning they are cheaper to launch and you can take more with you.

7 Reusable rockets

Fully reusable rockets will reduce the cost and difficulty of exploring further into space. In the future there could be a team of people stationed in Earth's orbit, supporting deep space missions.

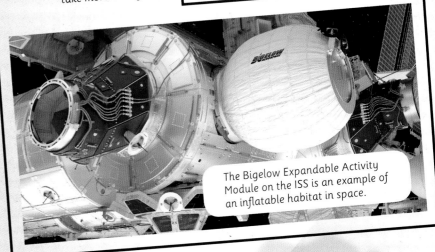

The Bigelow Expandable Activity Module on the ISS is an example of an inflatable habitat in space.

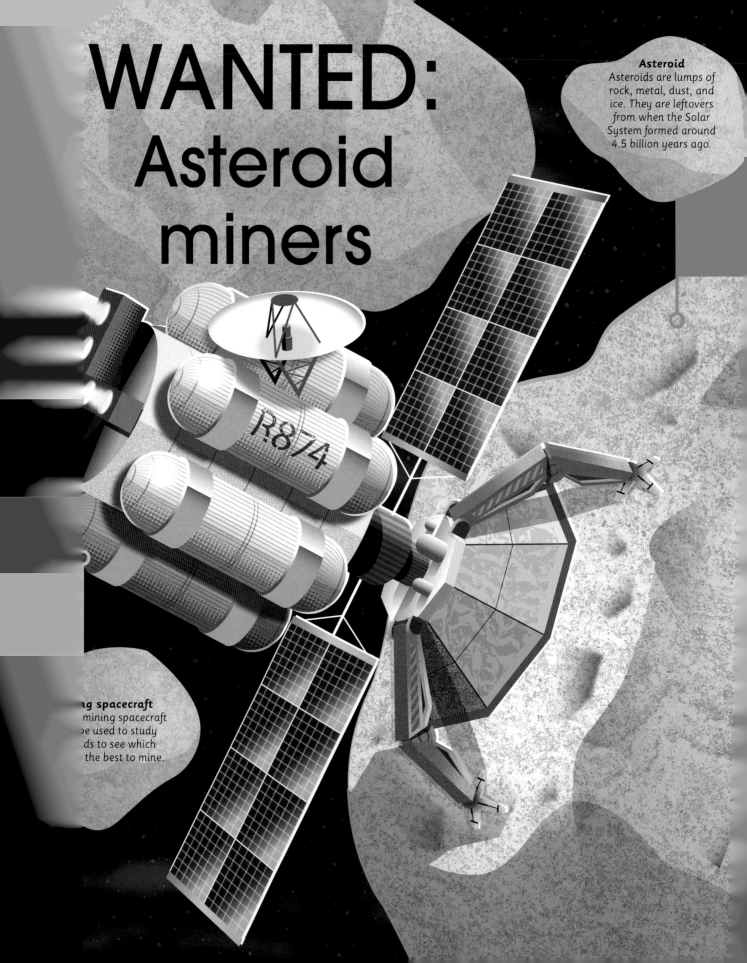

WANTED:
Asteroid miners

Asteroid
Asteroids are lumps of rock, metal, dust, and ice. They are leftovers from when the Solar System formed around 4.5 billion years ago.

...ng spacecraft
...mining spacecraft ...e used to study ...ds to see which ...the best to mine.

R8/4

For the past few years people have been trying to work out how they could mine for precious materials in space. Between the planets Mars and Jupiter lies the asteroid belt, where most of the asteroids in our Solar System live. This is a place with more than a million asteroids, some of which contain rare metals such as platinum and gold. Whoever succeeds in mining asteroids would become very wealthy.

However, becoming wealthy is not the main reason that people want to mine in space. Some of the asteroids, as well as the Moon, contain frozen water ice. Water is made up of the elements hydrogen and oxygen, things that are very important for space explorers as they can be converted into rocket fuel.

In the future, asteroids and the Moon could become a bit like petrol stations in space – allowing spacecraft to refuel before heading deeper into our Solar System.

OSIRIS-Rex

In 2017, NASA launched the OSIRIS-Rex spacecraft. Its mission is to visit an asteroid called Bennu, bring back a sample from the surface, and help scientists understand more about what asteroids are made of. The mission is also helping to develop important technologies for asteroid exploration, which will help future space miners.

Holidays in space

Since the beginning of the space race in the 1950s, people have dreamed of going on holiday to space. Today, that dream is almost a reality and some tourists have already gone on trips to the International Space Station (ISS).

In the near future, many more of us will get to go to space. Travel companies will take people on trips to space that last a few hours. The space tourists will be able to see the Earth from afar, and experience what it is like to feel weightless. However, the first trips will be extremely expensive.

What is happening now is not too different to when aeroplanes first started taking paying customers. To begin with, the trips cost a lot of money, but as aeroplane technology evolved and flights became cheaper, more people were able to take to the skies. The same will be true for space. One day in the future, people may be able to board a spacecraft to go on a holiday to another planet.

Destination:

In development

World View
Float up to the edge of space with World View. Enjoy fine dining and beautiful views from your balloon capsule, before gliding back to Earth.

Future destinations

Jupiter
★★★ **3,988 reviews**
Earth isn't the only planet where you can experience auroras. Jupiter also has these naturally occurring light displays and they are the greatest in the Solar System.

SPACE TOURIST

The first tourist in space was called Dennis Tito. In 2001, he paid $20 million for an eight-day trip to the ISS.

Blue Origin

Launch in the New Shepard capsule to more than 100 km (62 miles) above Earth. Experience 15 minutes of weightlessness before the capsule parachutes back down to Earth.

Virgin Galactic

Spend time in space aboard SpaceShipTwo. The spacecraft will be carried into the air by the WhiteKnightTwo aircraft, before being released mid-air and firing its rockets to get to space.

Titan

★★★★★ **2,895 reviews**

Fly to Saturn's largest moon, Titan, and experience how the Earth may have looked before life as we know it began.

Kepler-186f

★★★★★ **2,654 reviews**

Experience Kepler-186f — a planet outside of our Solar System that may have red grass!

As humans explore deeper into our Solar System and arrive at new moons or planets, they could use 3D printers to create everything they need using just the materials around them.

Instead of having to rely on supplies from Earth, astronauts will be able to make objects they need, like tools, parts for experiments, or medical kits. Creating things in space is essential if we want to travel far away from Earth.

Eventually, whole cities in space could be built this way. And delicate objects, which are extremely difficult to create on the ground due to gravity, could be 3D printed in space and then brought back to Earth.

How does 3D printing work?

A 3D printer on Earth normally uses plastic to build objects. The plastic is heated up so that it melts, and this melted plastic emerges from the printer's nozzle, building the object from the bottom upwards, layer after layer. As we explore different planets, we will find different materials that we can use for 3D printing.

3D-printed owl being made on Earth

Gravity meter

This gravity meter was the first privately funded object to be 3D printed in space. It is the first of many objects that companies will create in space in the future. A gravity meter is used by astronauts to signal when they reach weightlessness, as it will begin to float freely.

Printed tools

When astronaut Barry "Butch" Wilmore lost his wrench, instead of having to wait for another one to be brought from Earth, he was able to create a new one using a 3D printer on the ISS.

3D-printed wrench

Barry "Butch" Wilmore holding the 3D-printed wrench

Future spacesuits

NASA

This spacesuit is called the Z-2. It is being designed by NASA for future missions to Mars. It is lightweight, flexible, and will be able to withstand the harsh environment on the Red Planet. It has adjustable shoulders and waist, so it can fit people of all shapes and sizes!

SpaceX

This spacesuit is worn by astronauts inside SpaceX's Crew Dragon spacecraft. It is much less bulky than traditional spacesuits, but is not designed to be worn outside a spacecraft.

Spacesuits make the impossible possible. They allow people to survive outside a spaceship on spacewalks, walk on the Moon, and in the future they will enable people to walk on other planets. Spacesuits also have other uses, such as providing protection to astronauts in case of emergencies during launch and re-entry to Earth.

As our exploration of space continues, people will go where they have never been before, and will spend more time on places such as the Moon. As a result,

BioSuit™

Designed by Professor Dava Newman, the Massachusetts Institute of Technology (MIT) BioSuit™ is a skintight spacesuit that will act like a second skin for future astronauts. It's very light and will allow astronauts to move around easily in it.

Boeing

Here, astronaut Chris Ferguson is wearing the Boeing spacesuit, which is designed to be worn aboard Boeing's Starliner spacecraft. It weighs about 9 kg (20 lb), has a soft helmet and visor attached to the suit, and comes with touchscreen friendly gloves.

the spacesuits astronauts wear will evolve.

Modern spacesuits are still bulky, but future advances in technology could change this. Spacesuits of the future might fit better, weigh less, and be easier to move around in while still providing all the protection that astronauts will need.

Preparing for dust

One of the biggest problems for the Apollo astronauts was Moon dust. The suits that they wore got extremely dusty, but luckily the longest missions only lasted a few days. When astronauts return to the Moon for longer periods of time, they will need to wear suits that are resistant to Moon dust.

You may not realize it, but we are living in a world transformed by space. Although it might not be the space future that was imagined during the 1960s, we are living in a space age. From technology that relies on satellites in space to inventions made for space travel that are now being used on Earth, life is better because of space exploration.

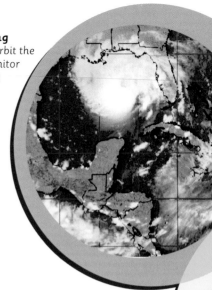

Weather forecasting
Some satellites that orbit the Earth are used to monitor the weather. They are able to make more accurate weather forecasts and closely study extreme weather events, such as hurricanes.

Space-age Earth life

NASTRAN
Developed by NASA engineers during the 1960s, NASTRAN software was used to design efficient space vehicles and to do structural analysis. Today, the same software is used to test big structures like aeroplanes, nuclear reactors, and even roller-coasters.

Firefighter gear

Flame-resistant materials developed by NASA for spacesuits are now used by firefighters to help keep them safe when putting out fires.

GPS

Satellites in space allow people to follow directions on sat-navs or use maps on a smartphone. In fact, if you own a smartphone, it regularly communicates with satellites!

Glasses and digital cameras

Scratch-resistant sun-filtering lenses came from research at NASA, as did the idea of digital cameras. The word "pixel" (short for picture element) was first used by NASA engineer Frederic Billingsley in 1965.

Medicine

Work with robotics on the ISS has influenced medical developments here on Earth. Robotic technology can now be used to assist with complicated operations.

Farming

Food and farming has benefited because of space. Satellite images have started to help some farmers better understand how their crops are growing and let them monitor their crops for diseases.

Why Mars?

The next major goal in the human exploration of space is Mars. In the past, this planet was probably much warmer and wetter. We have so many questions about Mars. Did life once exist there? Could life still exist in a simple form? If there was life on Mars, what happened to it? We've been asking these extraordinary questions for many centuries. To find the answers we need a lot of evidence.

While robots have helped us learn more about the Red Planet, they can't replace humans on the ground. If we want to know for sure if life once existed on Mars, the best way to find out is by visiting. And it's not just the possibility of life that's interesting – learning more about the geology of Mars could help us to understand more about how Earth and the other planets in the Solar System formed.

Size of Mars

Mars is smaller than Earth and like Earth, Mars has seasons. A year (the time it takes a planet to travel around the Sun) is much longer on Mars because it is further away from the Sun. However, a day (the time it takes for a planet to spin once on its axis) on Mars is similar in length to a day on Earth.

South pole
In 2018, ESA's Mars Express spacecraft discovered liquid water underneath Mars's south pole.

North pole
Like the Earth,
Mars has poles.
There is frozen
water ice at them.

Mars's surface
Mars is home to canyons,
dry riverbeds, and the largest
volcano in our Solar System –
Olympus Mons. Sometimes huge
dust storms run across the planet.
They pick up so much dust that they
can be seen by telescopes here on
Earth. Mars has an atmosphere,
but it is much thinner than
the Earth's, with no air
to breathe.

Olympus Mons

Phobos

Deimos

Two moons
Mars has two moons,
Phobos and Deimos, but
they are nothing like our
own Moon. They are small
and oddly shaped, and
were probably asteroids
that were pulled towards
Mars by its gravity.

One of the main reasons why we want to visit
Mars is to satisfy our curiosity. In the entire history
of humankind, the furthest distance we have travelled
in space is about 385,000 km (240,000 miles) – when we
went to the Moon. Putting humans on Mars would be the
beginning of our exploration further into the Solar System.

A mission to Mars isn't going to be easy. There are lots of challenges to overcome – such as radiation from the Sun and the effects of long periods of weightlessness on the human body. At the moment, government agencies, including NASA, and private companies are developing ideas for how to send people to the Red Planet.

Earth's position at landing on Mars

Earth

Mars's orbit

Earth's orbit

1

Leaving Earth
The crew will say goodbye to their friends and family as they begin their adventure. They may launch in a small spacecraft and meet with a larger vehicle that has been assembled in orbit.

2

Long journey
As the crew travel deeper into space, the Earth and the Moon will get smaller. They won't get bored – they will be busy looking after the spacecraft, exercising, and will have time off to watch films!

Earth

The journey to Mars
The journey to Mars will take at least six months. At its closest point, Mars is about 54 million km (34 million miles) from Earth. However, in the time it will take to travel there, Earth and Mars will move to different positions as they travel around the Sun.

4 **Landing on Mars**
As the spacecraft arrives at Mars, the astronauts may use a smaller spacecraft to travel to the surface.

Mars

Sun

Mars's position at launch

Mars

3
Communicating with mission control
As astronauts get further away from Earth, there will be a delay in their communications with mission control. Instead of radio contact, they may send recorded video messages back to Earth.

Touchdown

Landing on Mars is extremely difficult, and is nothing like landing on the Moon or Earth. This is because Mars has a thin atmosphere, which makes it hard for spacecraft to slow down on entry. Here are two artist's impressions of SpaceX's Dragon spacecraft landing on Mars.

SpaceX's Dragon spacecraft during landing

SpaceX's Dragon spacecraft after landing

Humans on Mars

Imagine travelling for at least six months across our Solar System and seeing Earth getting smaller and smaller until it is just a dot in the sky. You are now further away from home than any human has ever been in the history of our species. As you and your crew arrive at Mars, you see the dusty red landscape come into view.

Descending through the thin atmosphere, slowed first by a big parachute, then by rockets on your spacecraft, you eventually arrive safely on the surface. It will take you a few days to adjust to Mars's low gravity level, which is around one-third of Earth's gravity. Then, the time comes to put on your spacesuit, open the door of your spacecraft, and take the first steps on another planet.

Just as when Neil Armstrong and Buzz Aldrin set foot on the Moon, millions of people back on Earth will be watching as your boot touches the soil. You are now the first person to set foot on another planet. What would your first words be?

Sunset on Mars
On Mars the sky is pink-red, but the sunsets are blue. This photo was taken by the Curiosity rover, but one day people will get to witness these blue sunsets with their own eyes.

Living on Mars

One day, humans will live and work on Mars. However, unlike going to the Moon, a mission to Mars will result in more than just flags and footprints being left behind.

The goal is to have a permanent and continually occupied base on Mars. This base will be our first outpost on another planet, and will act as a stepping stone to help us explore even deeper into space. It will also bring us one step closer to becoming a multi-planetary species.

When we explored new places on Earth, we adapted to the land. We will need to do the same on Mars and use existing Martian resources to survive – this process is called "in-situ utilization". One of the most important resources on Mars is water ice. This could be used to make fuel, and even to make houses for astronauts to live in. Water ice could help protect astronauts from the dangers of radiation on the planet. The technology we need to do this is already being developed.

Growing food on Mars

Farming is important for space exploration as astronauts will need to grow food to survive away from Earth. As well as being a source of food, plants will also help to support the environment of a Mars base, converting the carbon dioxide we breathe out into the oxygen we need to breathe in.

Mars ice house
This igloo structure, designed by NASA, is inflatable and surrounded by a shell of water ice. It would need to be set up by robots before the astronauts arrive.

Insulation
A layer of carbon dioxide gas in the walls of the ice house can be used to control inside temperatures. This insulation will protect astronauts from the extreme Martian weather, and carbon dioxide is another resource that is available on Mars.

Are we alone?

Energy
Life on Earth would not be possible without the Sun, which is a constant source of energy.

Our planet
Earth is unique because it is the only place where we are certain that life exists.

Raw materials
Raw materials needed for life are found all over Earth – for example in soil.

Earth from far away
If a powerful planet-hunting telescope from far away was pointed at Earth, this is what it would look like.

Enceladus
A frozen moon of Saturn, Enceladus is believed to have a liquid ocean underneath its icy surface.

Europa
Orbiting around Jupiter, Europa has an icy surface with evidence of a liquid ocean beneath it.

Studying Earth
The universe is gigantic and there are lots of places we could look for life. Understanding more about the Earth, including the extreme places life can exist – such as deep beneath the ocean – helps to focus the search of where to look in space.

What you need for life

In order for life as we know it to exist, you need three basic ingredients: an energy source, liquid water, and raw materials – such as oxygen, nitrogen, and carbon. Scientists look for these three things when looking for life elsewhere.

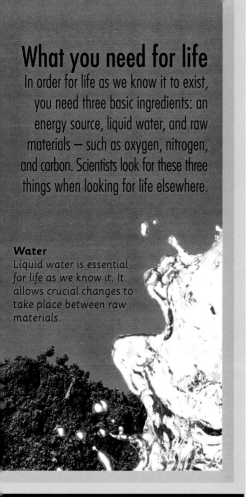

Water
Liquid water is essential for life as we know it. It allows crucial changes to take place between raw materials.

Life within our Solar System

Even if we don't discover life on Mars, there could still be life elsewhere in our Solar System. Among the places scientists are looking at are the moons around other planets.

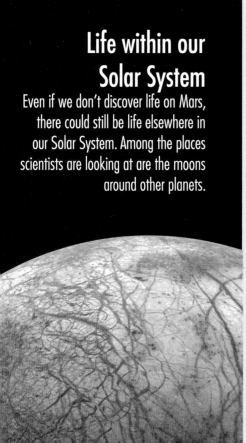

One of the biggest questions we are still yet to answer is "Are we alone?" At the moment, the only life we know of is here on Earth. We have not yet discovered aliens, and as far as we know, aliens have not discovered us!

We think it's unlikely that we are completely alone. Life can exist in some extreme places on Earth, and we also know that there are lots and lots of other planets in the universe. But until we find life – or it finds us – we won't know the answer for sure.

There may even be life elsewhere within our Solar System. If this is confirmed, it would mean that life would have developed by itself more than once in our Solar System, and that it is far more likely that life has evolved elsewhere in the Universe. Just imagine what else is out there.

"During **this century**, we will explore **moons** and **planets** in our Solar System with **robots and humans**, looking for life."
— Jill Tarter, scientist searching for extraterrestrial intelligence at the SETI Institute

Science non-fiction

Tablet
The 1960s TV series *Star Trek* was set in a future in which humans explored space. It featured tablet-like electronic clipboards.

Robotic arm
The sci-fi movie *2001: A Space Odyssey* was released in 1968. It predicted that future spacecraft would have robotic arms.

Dream

Dream

Tablet
Lots of people use a tablet today. It's a handheld computer that's ideal for using the internet, sending emails, and playing games.

Robotic arm
Robotic arms were first used in space in 1981. Today, there is one in use on the ISS, called Canadarm2.

Reality

Reality

For a long time, people have been dreaming up crazy ideas for the future. Sometimes these ideas come true! In fact, science fiction could be renamed "science prediction", because many of the things that people have imagined eventually turn into reality.

Sci-fi writers, scientists, and artists often think of things long before they happen. Whatever you dream up may seem impossible now, but it doesn't mean it always will be.

Some of the ideas imagined in the past were made fun of at the time.

Helicopter
In the late 15th century, the Italian artist and scientist Leonardo da Vinci came up with the idea of a helicopter-like machine.

Dream

Television
The first televisions were big and bulky. However, the characters in *The Jetsons* watched flat-screen TVs.

Dream

Robot
The Jetsons was a space-age cartoon series first released in 1962. The Jetson family had a robot to do household chores.

Reality

Helicopter
In 1907, the first helicopter-type aircraft flew for just one minute. Today, helicopters are used all around the world.

Reality

Television
Today, flat-screen TVs are in common use. They show much better quality images than old, bulky televisions.

Five hundred years ago, who would have believed that helicopters or robotic assistants could ever exist? But they now do.

The reality of these ideas isn't always *exactly* how people imagined, but that's part of the excitement too!

Robot
This robotic vacuum cleaner can whizz around cleaning your floors while you put your feet up.

Reality

Space jobs

There are lots of different jobs in the space industry – you don't just have to be an astronaut. Many thousands of people work from Earth to support both human and robotic missions.

In the future, as we explore further into space, there will be a lot of different jobs to do. We will need engineers to build space robots, travel agents to help book holidays in space, and doctors to help space travellers stay healthy.

The type of people who can go into space will also change. We will need to take people who are good at building and growing food. To make sure future space missions are successful they will also need to get on well with others.

WE WANT YOU!

Spacecraft designer

Imagine being able to design spacecraft for missions to the Moon, Mars, or perhaps even an asteroid. People already have jobs designing both robotic spacecraft and ones that can carry astronauts. As we travel further into space, skilled engineers and designers will be needed to create the next generation of spacecraft, able to take on new challenges.

Teacher

Every astronaut was inspired by a teacher, and today on board the ISS astronauts work with teachers back on Earth to help show children how exciting space travel is. Teaching others about space and STEM (science, technology, engineering, and maths) subjects is vital if we are to continue exploring. One day, in the future, lessons may even be held in orbit around the Earth, on the Moon, or even on Mars!

Find a job

Farmer

Future astronauts – particularly those who travel a long way from Earth – won't be able to rely solely on supplies. Having someone who is skilled at growing food will be vital for future space missions. One of the most important skills they will need to have is to be able to grow crops in extreme environments – such as on the Moon or in microgravity.

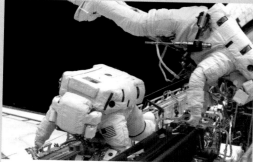

Builder

Astronauts were required to do spacewalks to build the ISS, and they still do spacewalks to carry out repairs. As humans go to the Moon and then Mars, they will need to take people with skills in building with them – to help construct future bases.

An interview with a Virgin Galactic test pilot

Kelly Latimer (centre)

Name: Kelly Latimer   **Job title:** Virgin Galactic test pilot

Q. How you got your job?
A. Before this job, I flew as a test pilot in the Air Force, with NASA, and then at Boeing. I had a lot of flight test experience in many different aircraft, which helped me to get this job with Virgin Galactic.

Q. What is so exciting about your job?
A. The possibility to go to space... a lot!

Q. How do I get a job like yours ?
A. It is important to get a good education, especially in maths and science. Then you need to build a lot of flying time in as many different aeroplanes as you can.

Q. What are your hopes for the future of space tourism?
A. At the moment, space tourism is something extraordinary that we are still working to achieve. I hope someday it is just a normal trip that everyone gets to take. I also hope it leads to more space exploration.

Future spaceships

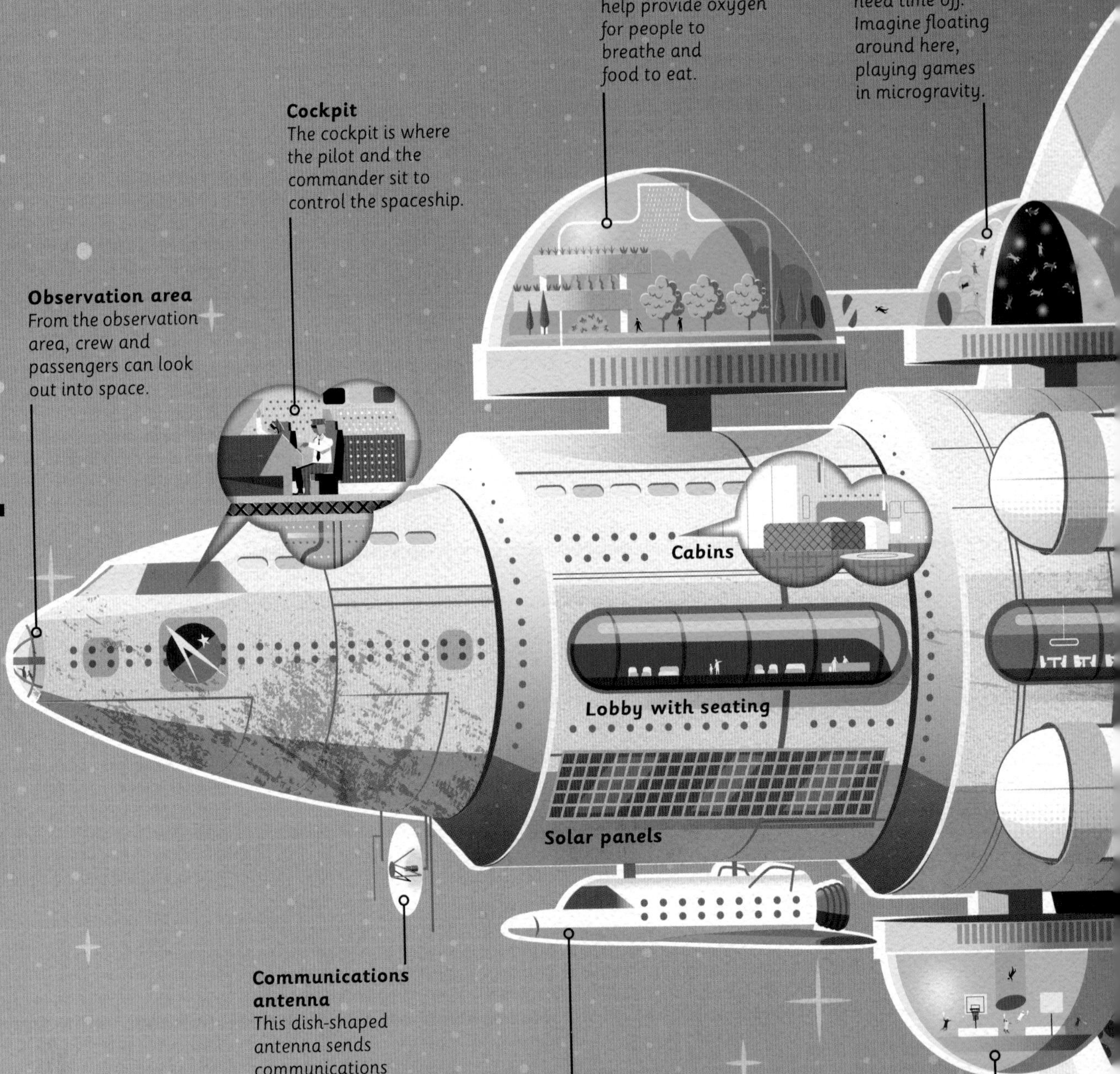

Plant dome
Plants grown here help provide oxygen for people to breathe and food to eat.

Recreation dome
Even astronauts need time off. Imagine floating around here, playing games in microgravity.

Cockpit
The cockpit is where the pilot and the commander sit to control the spaceship.

Observation area
From the observation area, crew and passengers can look out into space.

Cabins

Lobby with seating

Solar panels

Communications antenna
This dish-shaped antenna sends communications back to Earth.

Landing craft
This smaller spacecraft is used to take astronauts to the surface of other planets.

Sports dome
In the sports dome, astronauts can work out and play their favourite sports to keep fit and healthy.

Rotating gravitational ring
A rotating wheel in space will spin around to create artificial gravity. Wernher von Braun was one of the scientists who helped develop this concept.

Rocket boosters
These will help this spacecraft zoom across the Universe at super-fast speeds.

Fuel tanks

Restaurant

Observation areas

This spaceship isn't real, it has been imagined. It isn't just science and engineering that enable us to go to space, it is also creativity. This creativity allows us to think of new ideas and to solve tricky problems so that we are able to explore deeper into space. If you designed a future spaceship, what would it look like?

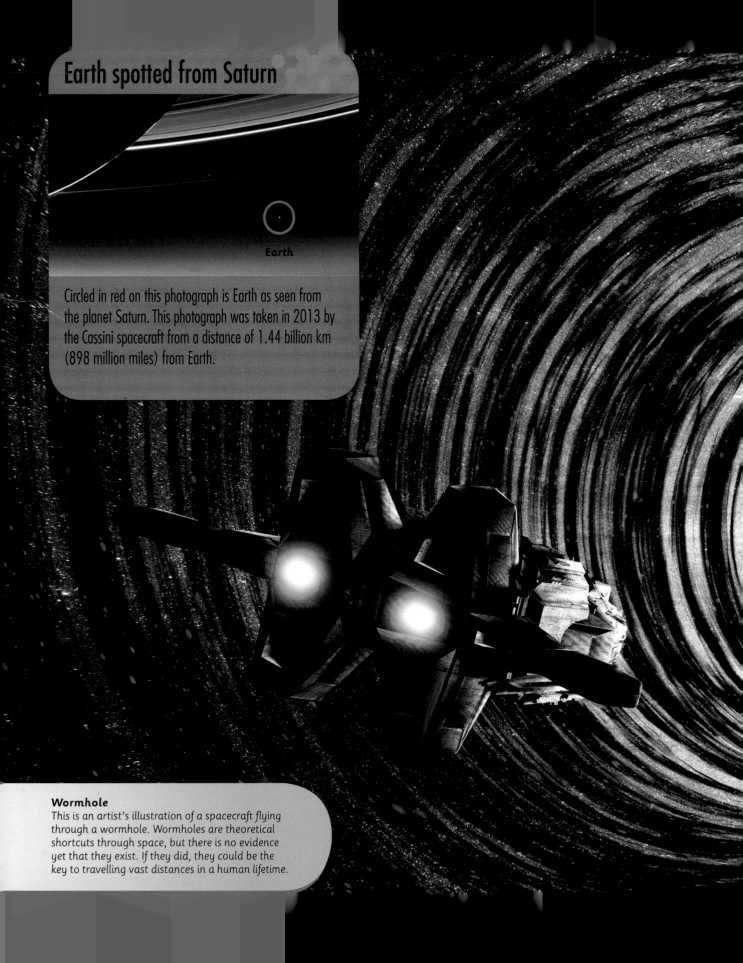

Earth spotted from Saturn

Earth

Circled in red on this photograph is Earth as seen from the planet Saturn. This photograph was taken in 2013 by the Cassini spacecraft from a distance of 1.44 billion km (898 million miles) from Earth.

Wormhole
This is an artist's illustration of a spacecraft flying through a wormhole. Wormholes are theoretical shortcuts through space, but there is no evidence yet that they exist. If they did, they could be the key to travelling vast distances in a human lifetime.

Voyage into space

There is a whole universe out there waiting to be explored. Earth is just one planet that orbits an average star (the Sun), in the corner of a galaxy, which is one of many billions of galaxies that exist.

One day humans will board a spacecraft and travel across our Solar System. Imagine looking out of the window and seeing Jupiter, or passing Pluto and its ice volcanoes. You could see comets up-close and look back at Earth, which would appear the same size as a star in the night sky. These are things that seem impossible now, but that won't always be the case.

Eventually people may even leave our Solar System and voyage deeper into space. In order to do this we will need to invent technology to travel faster, so that we can reach planets around other stars. Our space travel adventure is only just beginning.

Looking after
Spaceship Earth

No matter where we go in space, Earth will always be our home.

When you really think about it, planet Earth is a bit like a spaceship – and we are the passengers! More than 7 billion people, plus all other living things, share our spaceship home.

Space exploration is teaching us a lot about Earth. The satellites we've sent to space show us how the climate of our planet is changing, and it's not good news. Temperatures are rising faster than normal. This is because there are more harmful gases in the atmosphere as a result of pollution and forests being chopped down.

Travelling into space is the most significant thing humans will do as a species. Not just because of the adventure, but also because it changes our view of Earth. One day, people may live on other planets. However, Earth will always be our home. We all need to look after Spaceship Earth.

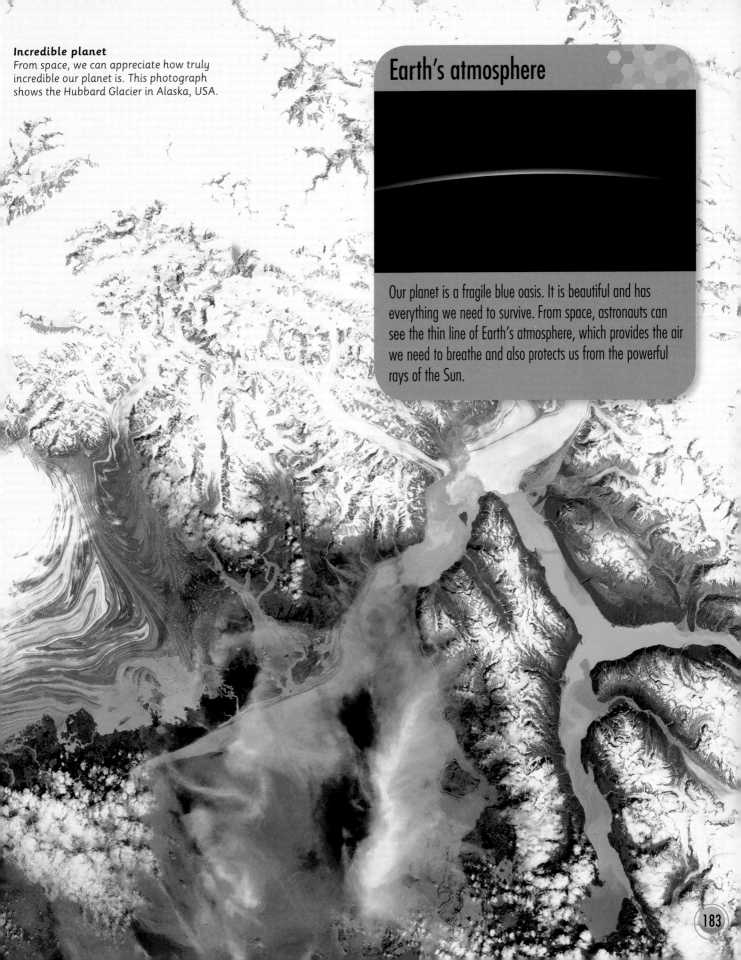

Incredible planet

From space, we can appreciate how truly incredible our planet is. This photograph shows the Hubbard Glacier in Alaska, USA.

Earth's atmosphere

Our planet is a fragile blue oasis. It is beautiful and has everything we need to survive. From space, astronauts can see the thin line of Earth's atmosphere, which provides the air we need to breathe and also protects us from the powerful rays of the Sun.

Footsteps into space

Throughout history, humans have achieved things they once thought were impossible. Little more than a century ago, to fly was just a dream. Since then, 12 people have walked on the Moon. Now, we mostly take flying for granted – and anyone born after November 2000 hasn't known a time when there weren't people continuously living and working in space.

As the rate of technology advances ever faster, so will our adventures in space. The Universe is yours to be discovered. It is not only as strange as you can imagine, it is stranger *than* you can imagine!

Humans will, in your lifetime, return to the Moon and then travel onwards to Mars. In fact, the first person to walk on Mars is probably in school right now.

In the words of Eugene Cernan, the last person to walk on the Moon: "Dream the impossible and go out and make it happen. I walked on the Moon – what can't you do?"

To be continued…

Footprint on Mars
This artist's impression shows
what the footprint of the first
person to walk on the surface
of Mars might look like.

Glossary

airlock
Small, sealed room where astronauts can enter or exit a spacecraft or space station

artificial
Created by humans

asteroid
Rocky object that orbits, or travels around, the Sun

astronaut
Human space traveller

atmosphere
Layer of gas that surrounds a planet

booster
Small rocket attached to a larger rocket to produce extra power during launch

comet
Object made of ice and dust, which develops a tail as it travels near to the Sun

Command/Service Module (CSM)
Crew cabin of the Apollo spacecraft, where astronauts lived and worked during their journey from the Earth to the Moon

cosmonaut
Russian equivalent of an astronaut

crew
Group of people who work on a spacecraft

dock
When a spacecraft joins with another spacecraft or space station in space

dwarf planet
Object that orbits the Sun, but which is too small to be classed as a planet

ESA
European Space Agency

exoplanet
Planet that orbits a star other than the Sun

galaxy
Huge group of stars, dust, and gas held together by gravity

gravity
Force that pulls objects towards each other

Kuiper belt
Ring of ice and rock that is beyond Neptune

laboratory
Place where science experiments are done

launch
Process of using rockets to send something into space

lunar
Word that relates to the Moon

Lunar Module (LM)
Part of the Apollo spacecraft that landed on the Moon

meteorite
Piece of rock, metal, or ice that lands on a planet or moon's surface

microgravity
When the force of gravity is present, but its effect is small. Microgravity causes objects to become weightless in space

Milky Way
Galaxy we live in

module
Part of a space station that can be connected to other parts

moon
Object that orbits a planet or asteroid

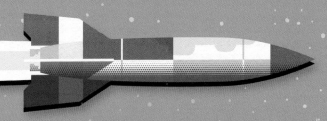

NASA
US space agency. NASA stands for National Aeronautics and Space Administration

nebula
Cloud of dust and gas in space where stars are born

orbit
Path an object takes around another when pulled by its gravity — for example, the Moon orbits the Earth

payload
Cargo carried into space by a rocket. It may include supplies, spacecraft, or satellites

planet
Large, spherical object that orbits a star

probe
Uncrewed robotic spacecraft designed to study objects in space and send information back to Earth

radiation
Rays of energy, which can be harmful

Red Planet
Nickname of the planet Mars, because of its red-coloured, rusty soil

rendezvous
Meet up at an agreed time and place

rocket
Machine that can propel itself into space

rover
Vehicle that is driven on the surface of a moon or a planet that is not Earth

satellite
Object that orbits another larger object

simulation
Controlled test of a situation that might be encountered — for example, doing experiments on the Moon

solar
Word that relates to the Sun

Solar System
The Sun and everything that orbits it

space station
Large spacecraft where astronauts live and do experiments

spacecraft
Vehicle that travels in space

spacesuit
Specially designed sealed clothing worn by an astronaut to protect them in space

spacewalk
When an astronaut in space is outside a spacecraft, usually to repair or test equipment

star
Huge, glowing sphere of gas, such as the Sun

telescope
Tool used to look at faraway objects

test pilot
Pilot who flies aircraft to test that they work

tether
Cord that attaches an astronaut to a spacecraft during a spacewalk

Universe
All of space and everything in it

wormhole
Theoretical passage in space that can connect two places that are great distances apart

Index

Acknowledgements

About the author

Sarah Cruddas is a British space journalist, broadcaster, and author with an academic background in astrophysics. She is a regular face on TV in the UK, as well as writing and speaking globally about why space exploration matters. Sarah believes that the exploration of space is the most significant thing we will ever do as a species and hopes to inspire the next generation of scientists, engineers, and astronauts.

Great endeavours require a great team and Sarah would like to thank the team at DK for helping make this book possible. In particular Sam Priddy, Lucy Sims, and Katie Lawrence for all their hard work, time, and patience. And Sarah Larter for believing in this idea. Thank you to everyone who agreed to be interviewed for this book. Additional thanks to Julie and Andrew McDermott at Space Lectures, Emily Holmes, Kathi Schmier, and everyone else who offered help and support.

This book is dedicated to every single person that works to make space exploration possible. We owe our future to you.

Dorling Kindersley would like to thank Jaileen Kaur for coordinating the hi-res images, Caroline Hunt for proofreading, and Helen Peters for the index.

The Gene Cernan quotes on pp. 90–91 and 184–185 are from *The Last Man on the Moon*

Quotes: pp. 32–33 John F. Kennedy, Rice University Stadium speech, 12 September 1962;
© Mark Stewart Productions.

The publisher would like to thank the following for their kind permission to reproduce their photographs:

(Key: a-above; b-below/bottom; c-centre; f-far; l-left; r-right; t-top)

6 Alamy Stock Photo: NG Images (cl). NASA: JSC (cla, bl); KSC (tl). 8-9 NASA. 12-13 NASA: JPL-Caltech (bc). 13 NASA: ESA. 16 Alamy Stock Photo: D Hale-Sutton (tl). Getty Images: thipjang (cla). 16-17 Alamy Stock Photo: Science History Images (tc). 17 Alamy Stock Photo: Granger Historical Picture Archive (tl); Science History Images (cr). 18 Alamy Stock Photo: Granger Historical Picture Archive (c). 19 Alamy Stock Photo: Chronicle (cl); Granger Historical Picture Archive (tl); Moviestore collection Ltd (bc); World History Archive (cr). Getty Images: SVF2 (cra). NASA: MSFC (crb). 21 Getty Images: Hulton Archive (bc); Topical Press Agency / Stringer (clb). NASA: MSFC (ca). 22 NASA: MSFC. 23 Science Photo Library: Sputnik. 24 Alamy Stock Photo: Granger Historical Picture Archive (c). Getty Images: Chronicle (br). 25 Getty Images: Bettmann (br); Bill ullstein bild Dtl. (tl); Space prime (bc). 28-29 NASA. 30 Alamy Stock Photo: Heritage Image Partnership Ltd (l); SPUTNIK (r). 31 akg-images: Sputnik (c). NASA: MSFC (br). 32 Getty Images: Bob Gomel / The LIFE Images Collection. 34-35 Getty Images: Sovfoto / UIG (c). 35 Alamy Bridges / The LIFE Images Collection (bl). 26 Alamy Stock Photo: ITAR-TASS News Agency (t). Getty Images: Sovfoto / UIG (c). 27 Alamy Stock Photo: Granger Historical Picture Archive (r). Stock Photo: ITAR-TASS News Agency (cra, cr); Sputnik (br). 38-39 Science Photo Library: Sputnik (c). 38 Getty Images: Bettmann (clb). 40-41 NASA. 40 NASA: (tr). 42 Alamy Stock Photo: Netflix / Courtesy Everett Collection Inc (br). NASA: (clb). 43 Courtesy of the International Women's Air & Space Museum , Cleveland, Ohio: (l). Getty Images: Bettmann (tc/Jerrie Cobb); Thomas D. Mcavoy (ca/Mary Wallace Funk, clb); Time Life Donald Uhrbrock / The LIFE Images Collection (tc); Shel Hershorn / The LIFE Images Collection (cla, bc); Nat Farbman / The LIFE Picture Collection (ca); Don Cravens / The LIFE Images Collection (cla/JETSONS); Joe Tree (tr); INTERFOTO (cr). Dorling Kindersley: Museum of Design in Plastics, Bournemouth Arts University, UK (bl). Pictures (cra); The Denver Post (cl, bl). NASA: (tr). 44 Alamy Stock Photo: Everett Collection Inc (cr). Dorling Kindersley: Parker Harris Collection (bl). Dreamstime.com: Christoph Weihs / Aeolos (tr). Getty Images: Universal History Archive / UIG (tl). 46 NASA: Brad Ball / Langley Research Center (tc); (d, cr, bc). 47 NASA: JSC (bl, br, tl, tr); Bob Nye / NASA Langley Research Center (c). 48 Dreamstime.com: Smithsonian National Air and Space Museum: NASM 9A14823 (bc). 45 Alamy Stock Photo: Trinity Mirror / Mirrorpix (c); Old Visuals (tr/Unisphere). NASA: (c). Rex by Shutterstock: (tc). 55 Alamy Stock Photo: NASA Image Nerthuz (tr). 50-51 NASA: JSC. 51 NASA: Kennedy Space Center, FL (cr). NASA: (cla, ca). 57 NASA: (tl, cra); Moss (cla). 58 NASA: Ed Hengeveld (clb). 61 Science Photo Library: Babak Tafreshi (tr). 62-63 NASA. 63 NASA: (tr). Collection (ca). NASA: JSC (tl, tr). 56 Alamy Stock Photo: Archive PL (cra). NASA: (cla, ca). 67 Getty Images: Ralph Morse / The LIFE Picture Collection (cra). NASA: Saturn Apollo Program (c). 68 NASA: Image 64 NASA: (tr); KSC (bl). 65 NASA: (cr); KSC (tl). 66-67 NASA: (c). 66 NASA: Great Images in NASA (c); (cl). 69 NASA: Image Science and Analysis Laboratory, NASA-Johnson Space Center. (tr). 70-71 NASA. 72 Getty Images: Bob Peterson / The LIFE Science and Analysis Laboratory, NASA-Johnson Space Center. (c, br); Kipp Teague. (cl). 73 Getty Images: Bettmann (tr); The Sydney Morning Herald / Trevor Dallen / Fairfax Images Collection (tc); Evening Standard / Stringer (bl). 72-73 Alamy Stock Photo: Tor Eigeland (bc). NASA: (c). Rex by Shutterstock: (tc). 81 Alamy Stock Photo: NASA Photo (tl). Getty Media (br). 74 NASA: JSC (ca, tl, tr). 75 NASA: Image Science and Analysis Laboratory, NASA-Johnson Space Center. (tr);. 76 Getty Images: © ABC (tl). 77 NASA: (tr); KSC (cla). 81 Alamy Stock Photo: NASA Photo (tl). Getty Images: Bettmann (d, cb); Keystone-France / Gamma-Rapho (tr); Keystone-France\Gamma-Rapho (cr); Time Life Pictures / NASA / The LIFE Picture Collection (bl); George Lipman / The Sydney Morning Herald / Fairfax Media (crb). 82 NASA: JSC (b, tl, tr). 83 NASA: JSC (tl, cl, bl, tr, cr, br). 84 Getty Images: Hulton-Deutsch Collection / CORBIS (tr). 85 William Suitor. 87 NASA: (cra). 88-89 NASA. 90-91 NASA: Eugene A. Cernan (b). 91 NASA: (cr, tc). 92 NASA: (cla). Smithsonian National Air and Space Museum: TMS A19760745000cp02 (cra). 93 NASA: Goddard Space Flight Center (cla); (cra, tc). 96 NASA: Ed Hengeveld (cr); (c). 97 NASA: JSC (d, cr). 98-99 NASA: Davis Goddard Space Flight Center / ASU (c). 95 Alamy Stock Photo: National Geographic Image Collection (crb). NASA: J.L. Pickering (tl, tc); JSC (bc, bl, tr, c). 96 NASA: Ed Hengeveld (cr); (c). 97 NASA: JSC (d, cr). 98-99 NASA: Davis Meltzer / JSC. 99 NASA: (tl, crb). 100 Alamy Stock Photo: Sputnik (ca, cra). 100-101 Getty Images: Keystone-France / Gamma-Rapho (tr). NASA: JPL (tl, bl, c); (bc). 104 NASA: JSC (d). 105 NASA: AFRC Sputnik (cra). 102 NASA: JPL-Caltech / KSC (c); JPL (cr, br, cb); JPL / USGS (crb). 102-103 NASA: JPL (c). 103 Alamy Stock Photo: J Marshall - Tribaleye Images (tr). NASA: KSC (tr). Rex by Shutterstock: Denis Cameron (bl). 108 NASA: JSC (br). 109 NASA: JSC (tr); MSFC. (tr). 106 NASA: JSC. 106-107 NASA: JSC (tc). 107 Alamy Stock Photo: ITAR-TASS News Agency (bc); Sputnik (br). NASA: KSC (tr). 112 NASA: (tl, tr); MSFC (c). 113 NASA: (bl, tr). 114-115 NASA: (tc). 114 NASA: 111 NASA: ESA, and STScI (cr); JSC (tr); X-ray: CXC / PSU / L.Townsley et al.; Optical: STScI; Infrared: NASA / JPL / PSU / L.Townsley et al. (bl). 112 NASA: (tl, tr); MSFC (c). 113 NASA: (bl, tr). 114-115 NASA: (tc). 114 NASA: (tr); KSC. 115 NASA: JSC (tr, bc); MSFC (br). 117 NASA: (crb, bc). 118 ESA: NASA (clb). NASA: JSC (cr). 119 ESA: NASA (bl). NASA: JSC (crb, tl, cra). 120 NASA: Bill Ingalls. 121 NASA: Bill Ingalls (cl); JSC (tl). 122-123 NASA. 122 NASA: JSC (cb). 123 NASA: (crb). 124-125 NASA: (b). 124 NASA: (c). 125 NASA: (c); Karl Shreeves (br). 126 Alamy Stock Photo: Wang Jianmin / Xinhua (tr). NASA: Johns Hopkins University Applied Physics Laboratory / Carnegie Institution of Washington (crb). 127 ESA: NASA / JPL / University of Arizona (tc). NASA: JPL-Caltech / KSC / LEGO (cra); JPL (c); Goddard Space Flight Center (tl); JPL-Caltech / SwRI / Betsy Asher Hall / Gervasio Robles (clb); JPL-Caltech / Space Science Institute (c). 128 NASA: JPL-Caltech / MSSS. 129 NASA: Goddard Space Flight Center (br). 130 NASA: ESA, and M. Buie (c); Southwest Research Institute (tr); Johns Hopkins University Applied Physics Laboratory / Southwest Research Institute (c). 131 NASA: JPL (cb); JHUAPL / SwRI (c, tr). 132-133 Alamy Stock Photo: Krisikorn Tawrattanakul. NASA: JPL-Caltech (c). 132 NASA: Ames / JPL-Caltech / T. Pyle (t). 133 NASA: Ames / JPL-Caltech (tr, crb). 136 Getty Images: Bryan Chan / Los Angeles Times (br); Robert Laberge (crb). 137 ESA: J.Huart (bc). Getty Images: Pallava Bagla / Corbis (cr). NASA: Bill Ingalls (tl). 138-139 NASA: Robert Markowitz & Bill Stafford (c). 138 NASA: (tl, ca). 139 NASA: (cr, tc). 142 Alamy Stock Photo: Science Collection. 143 Alamy Stock Photo: Science Collection (c/S9, c/S10); Science Collection (d, d/S7, c). 144 Alamy Stock Photo: Bob Daemmrich (l). Getty Images: SpaceX / Handout (bc). 145 Alamy Stock Photo: Blue Origin (bc). Getty Images: Paul Morigi / WireImage (c). 146 NASA: (clb). 147 ESA: David Ducros, 2016 (tr). 148 Getty Images: VCG. 149 Alamy Stock Photo: Alejandro Miranda (br). Getty Images: AFP / STR (tc); VCG (tl). 150-151 ESA: Foster + Partners (t). 151 NASA: Regan Geeseman (br). 152 NASA: Scott Kelly (tr). 152-153 NASA: (c). 153 NASA: Bigelow Aerospace (br); ESA / SOHO (tr). 155 NASA: Dimitri Gerondidakis (cr). 156 NASA: (clb). 157 Alamy Stock Photo: Blue Origin (bc). Made In Space, Inc.: (bc/ratchet). NASA: (cb, crb). 158 Dreamstime.com: Mari1408 (bl, bc, bc/Owl). 158-159 Made In Space, Inc: Dylan Taylor 159 ESA / Hubble: NASA/Nick Rose/http://creativecommons.org/licenses/by/3.0 (bc). World View Enterprises, Inc.: (cra). 157 Alamy Stock Photo: Dennis MacDonald (tr). Dreamstime.com: Paul 160 NASA: SpaceX / KSC (cr); Bill Stafford (tr). 161 Copyright The Boeing Company /Boeing Images: (tr). Joshua Dalsimer; Dava Newman (cr). NASA: (crb). 162 Alamy Stock Photo: Dennis MacDonald (tr). Dreamstime.com: Paul Lemke / Lokinthru (c). 163 123RF.com: Kostic Dusan (cr). Alamy Stock Photo: BSIP SA (cb); Alex Segre (cl); Aleksey Zakirov (tr). Dorling Kindersley: Richard Leeney / Bergen County, NJ, Law and Public Safety Institute (tc). 164-165 NASA. 164 NASA: JPL (br). 165 NASA: JPL-Caltech / University of Arizona (crb). 167 Alamy Stock Photo: Science Collection (cr, br). 168 NASA: JPL / Cornell. 169 NASA: JPL-Caltech / MSSS / Texas A&M Univ. 174 Dreamstime. 170-171 NASA: Clouds AO / SEArch. 171 NASA: University of Arizona (tr). 172 NASA: JPL-Caltech / Space Science Institute (br); (d, t). 173 Dreamstime.com: Okea (c). NASA: JSC (cr). 175 123RF.com: Micha? Giel / gielmichal (br/ com: Jf123 / iPad is a trademark of Apple Inc., registered in the U.S. and other countries. (d). Getty Images: CBS Photo Archive (cla). NASA: Hulton Archive (cla). NASA: ESA, and the Hubble Heritage (STScI / AURA)-ESA / Hubble Collaboration tv). Alamy Stock Photo: Hanna-Barbera / Everett Collection (cra). Dreamstime.com: Colette6 (tl) / Duskbabe (cr). Getty Images: Hulton Archive (cla). NASA: ESA, and the Hubble Heritage (STScI / AURA)-ESA / Hubble Collaboration (br). 176 NASA: KSC (bl). Science Photo Library: (tr). 177 NASA: (cr); KSC (tl, bl). Virgin Galactic: (cra). 180-181 Getty Images: Matjaz Slanic / E+. 180 NASA: JPL-Caltech / Space Science Institute (cla). 182-183 NASA: Earth Observatory. 183 NASA: (cra). 184-185 NASA: JSC. Cover images: Front and Back: Dreamstime.com: Igor Marusitsenko (background)

All other images © Dorling Kindersley
For further information see: www.dkimages.com